UP

S0-ABB-126

disciple

LIFE • FREEDOM • PURPOSE

FREEDOM
IN CHRIST

Published by Monarch Books

an imprint of

Lion Hudson plc

Wilkinson House, Jordan Hill Road,

Oxford OX2 8DR, England

Email: monarch@lionhudson.com

www.lionhudson.com/monarch

ISBN: 978 0 85721 701 1

ISBN: 978 0 85721 702 8 (pack of five)

E-ISBN: 978 0 85721 703 5

First edition 2016

A catalogue record for this book is available from the British Library

Printed and bound in the UK, March 2016, LH26

Acknowledgments

All Scripture quotations, unless otherwise indicated, are taken from the Holy Bible, New International Version®, NIV®. Copyright ©1973, 1978, 1984, 2011 by Biblica, Inc.™ Used by permission of Zondervan. All rights reserved worldwide. www.zondervan.com The "NIV" and "New International Version" are trademarks registered in the United States Patent and Trademark Office by Biblica, Inc.™

Scripture quotations marked ESV are taken from The Holy Bible, English Standard Version® (ESV®), copyright © 2001 by Crossway, a publishing ministry of Good News Publishers. Used by permission. All rights reserved.

Scripture quotations marked NLT are taken from the Holy Bible, New Living Translation, copyright ©1996, 2004, 2007, 2013 by Tyndale House Foundation. Used by permission of Tyndale House Publishers, Inc., Carol Stream, Illinois 60188. All rights reserved.

Scripture marked NASB are taken from the NEW AMERICAN STANDARD BIBLE®, Copyright © 1960,1962,1963,1968,1971,1972,1973,1975,1977,1995 by The Lockman Foundation. Used by permission.

Contents

Credits and thanks

Our grateful thanks go to Dr. Neil T. Anderson, the Founder of Freedom In Christ Ministries, whose amazing teaching inspired *disciple*, and to the 69 individuals who made donations to enable this project to get off the ground. Without you, *disciple* would never have happened. Thanks too to the amazing team who worked on the project:

Producer: Steve Goss

Writers: Steve Goss, Jess Regnart, Dan Lodge, David Edwards, Rob Peabody, André Adefope

Design concepts: Jon Smethurst

Coffee Shop Films:

Presenters: David Edwards, Rob Peabody, Jess Regnart, André Adefope

Logistics: Rob Davies, Zoë Goss

Production (UCB Broadcast):

Andrew Walkington, Executive Producer

Ben Emery, Director

Malcolm Salt, Production Manager

Mark Tennant, Audio Engineer

Morgan Griffith, Audio Engineer

Luke Campbell, Camera Operator

Naomi Chandler, Camera Operator

Becky Welford, Camera Operator

Set design and dressing: Benn Price, Ben Poole, Sam Frawley, Amy Meadham

Set building: Roy Emery, Hugh Graham, Mark Kirshaw, Ryan Downes

Starter Films:

Presenter: Dan Lodge

Director: Rick Holland (Blink Media)

US Testimony Filming:

Co-ordinator: Trenidy Davis

Production of the written material:

Editor: Jenny Ward

Layout: Steve Goss

App design:

All round genius: Daniel Upton

Picture Credits

p.38 FreeImages.com/s s

p.49 FreeImages.com/Martin BOULANGER

p.55 FreeImages.com/Rene Asmussenfoto

p.81 FreeImages.com/Yazıcı Ekrem

p.85 FreeImages.com/Alexander Popelier

p.98 FreeImages.com/John Evans

p.109 FreeImages.com/Steve Knight

p.140 FreeImages.com/John Nyberg

p.153 FreeImages.com/Mike Bamford

p.154 FreeImages.com/Einar Hansen

p.165 FreeImages.com/Vicky Johnson

So, why disciple?

Disciple: One who is learning to become more and more like Jesus.

disciple is about your story and how it is intertwined with the greatest story ever told – God's story. It will take you on a journey to understand your life's real purpose.

No matter what has happened up to now, God has an amazing and unique plan for you, things prepared specifically for *you*. But whether or not God's plan actually works out for you is totally in your hands.

It's not about "trying harder", striving to follow God. It starts with knowing Him, knowing yourself, and knowing your role in the greatest story ever told.

You will discover that, because you are a new creation in Jesus, a holy one, nothing – *nothing!* – can hold you back from being all that God wants you to be. You really can ensure that your life makes a real difference, a difference that will have *eternal* consequences.

But it's not a foregone conclusion. There is plenty of stuff that tries to get in the way – and will if you let it. The world, the flesh, and the devil conspire to trip you up, fool you, and make you believe that you can never be free or make your life count. If you want God's story to be your story, it's crucial that you wise up to how they work.

disciple will help you work out what is getting in the way and deal with it so that you can be free – free to write the story that God wants you to write.

God's story starts with freedom. It finishes with radical transformation – Jesus in you, you in Jesus. Take hold of your freedom. Discover your mandate. Go out there in the power of the Holy Spirit. Make a difference that will last for ever.

Enjoy the ride!

Get the most from disciple

This Participant's Guide is designed to be used during *disciple* and is your own personal guide and journal. Please make it your own – there is plenty of space for you to write – and use it to record this part of your story. Here are six key ways to enure that *disciple* is a life-transforming experience rather than just an interesting course:

- Do your best to attend each session because each one builds on what has gone before. If you do have to miss one, do everything you can to catch up (perhaps by borrowing the DVDs if available).

- How much you get out of *disciple* will be in direct proportion to how intentional you are in taking hold of the principles taught, so try to engage with *disciple* between sessions. Use the "Going deeper" sections. Take time out to pray through what you learn.

- Get the *disciple* app (see page 7), which will give you something extra every day. You will also be able to watch the Starter Film with Dan before each session and consider the corresponding questions. It will give you access to six extra teaching films on key topics from Rob, Jess, and David (see pages 177–189).

- Much of what you learn will come from the people going through *disciple* with you. Participate in the discussions and try to encourage others during those times. Take the risk to be open and vulnerable but take care to share appropriately.

- Ensure you take the opportunity to go through *The Steps To Freedom In Christ*, a kind and gentle process that will help you "do business" with God. It comes between Sessions 8 and 9, is a critical part of *disciple*, and is absolutely not to be missed.

- *disciple* is designed to help you uncover any areas in your belief system that don't line up with what God tells us is actually true. At the end of every session record any faulty beliefs you become aware of on pages 190–191. In Session 9 you will be taught how to renew your mind to resolve them.

Connect with us

The *disciple* app contains a heap of helpful additional input as you progress through *disciple:*

- Six extra teaching films with Rob, Jess, and David
- Truth Encounter lists at your fingertips
- Create your own "Stronghold-Buster" and get daily reminders to use it
- Watch the Starter Film before each session.

Search for "disciple – Freedom In Christ" in your app store.

Join the *disciple* Facebook group
- Share your thoughts, questions, and stories
- Keep up to date with the world of Freedom In Christ
- From Facebook, search for "disciple", select the "closed group", and ask to join.

Find your local Freedom In Christ website
We operate in around 40 countries. Find your nearest office or representative at www.ficminternational.org.
- Our US site is at: www.ficm.org
- Our UK site is at: www.ficm.org.uk
Register on our UK site to receive our daily devotional by email.

DAVID EDWARDS was born on the sunny island of Trinidad in the Caribbean where he spent most of his formative years. He moved to the UK as a teenager and started a career in health and social care management. In 2010 David answered his call to full time pastoral ministry and resigned from his career. He currently pastors a congregation in Cheshire, England, where he lives with his wife, Linda, and their foster son Joshua. He is also the University Chaplain of Manchester Metropolitan University, where he gives pastoral support to both staff and students. David loves singing and was once runner-up in the London "Soloist of the Year" competition.

JESS REGNART works for Freedom In Christ Ministries equipping church leaders to disciple teenagers and young adults. Having grown up in an atheist/agnostic household she knows first-hand how hard it is to live without knowing God. After something of a Damascus road conversion in her early twenties she fell head over heels for Jesus and went on to complete a theology degree. Jess has a huge passion to help teenagers and young adults meet Jesus and see Him for who He really is. She also has a large shoe collection, loves Miss Piggy, hates bananas, and is learning to longboard with her dog.

ROB PEABODY serves as the Cofounder and International Director of Awaken, a non-profit organization that exists to resource the Church for action. In 2011, Rob, along with his wife, Medea, and their two boys, left his position as lead campus pastor of a megachurch in Texas, USA, to pioneer fresh expressions of church seeking to engage unreached 20s and 30s in northeast London, UK. He leads the International Mission Board, and heads up Fresh Expressions' pioneering efforts amongst the next generation. Rob has written multiple books and film resources (more info at awakenmovement.com). Rob is a fanatic about cinnamon ice cream, once got escorted by state troopers out of the Texas Governor's office after hours, cycled from London to Paris in 2013, and is definitely not a morning person.

DAN LODGE works as part of the resources team for Youth for Christ. His passion is to see churches equip young people to be able to go and share their faith. His role sees him creating resources for 11–25s as well as travelling and speaking all over the place. He has a hatred of tomatoes and loves nothing more than being spoken about in the third person.

ANDRÉ ADEFOPE (who features in the extra film on *The Gift Of Sex*) became a Christian at a talk entitled "sex before marriage" having previously struggled with self-image issues, being let down by friends, and romantic disasters. He has a keen interest in helping people apply God's Word to the area of dating and singleness. He is Head of Relationship Development at Visible Ministries in Manchester, UK, and oversees the "Relationship Dilemma" project. He is also an undefeated table tennis champion (though only in the Visible office).

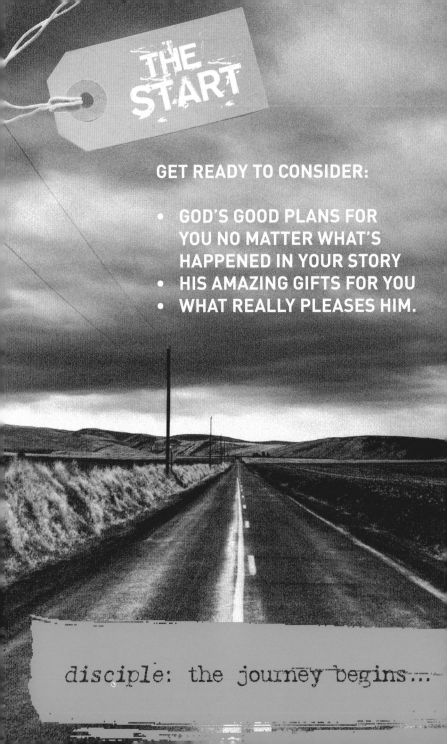

THE START

GET READY TO CONSIDER:

- GOD'S GOOD PLANS FOR YOU NO MATTER WHAT'S HAPPENED IN YOUR STORY
- HIS AMAZING GIFTS FOR YOU
- WHAT REALLY PLEASES HIM.

disciple: the journey begins...

Your unwritten autobiography

WHY?

For we are God's handiwork, created in Christ Jesus to do good works, which God prepared in advance for us to do.

Ephesians 2:10

If you are a Christian, you already have everything you need for your life story to make an impact that will last for ever.

What story are you going to write?

ONE WAY

When you were young, what did you want to be when you grew up?

How realistic do you think it is to imagine that your life from this point on could make a genuinely positive impact in the world?

Outrageous plans:

"For I know the plans I have for you," declares the Lord, "plans to prosper you and not to harm you, plans to give you hope and a future."

Jeremiah 29:11

God has a superb, outrageously amazing plan for your life which he planned for you before you were even born.

According to sociologists our generation is more self-obsessed than any generation that has come before.

Even when you get all the material and worldly things you think you want – there is still a void, a sense of pointlessness.

Narcissism:
inordinate fascination with oneself; excessive self-love; vanity. Synonyms: self-centeredness, smugness, egocentrism. (dictionary.com)

Chat

Thinking about what you wanted to be when you grew when you were a child, did this change over the years? If so, why did it change?

Looking to the future, if you were to list three things you want from the rest of your life, what would they be?

Outrageous love –
Outrageous grace

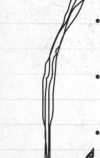

- You already have everything you need to make your life count for eternity and fulfil the plans God has for you – if you have become a child of God.
- God likes, delights, and loves you unconditionally no matter what you have done or might do in the future.
- No one has a back story too bad or messed up to become the person God created them to be and make their life count!

The Parable of the Lost Son

Jesus continued: "There was a man who had two sons. The younger one said to his father, 'Father, give me my share of the estate.' So he divided his property between them. "Not long after that, the younger son got together all he had, set off for a distant country and there squandered his wealth in wild living. After he had spent everything, there was a severe famine in that whole country, and he began to be in need. So he went and hired himself out to a citizen of that country, who sent him to his fields to feed pigs. He longed to fill his stomach with the pods that the pigs were eating, but no one gave him anything.

"When he came to his senses, he said, 'How many of my father's hired men have food to spare, and here I am starving to death! I will set out and go back to my father and say to him: Father, I have sinned against heaven and against you. I am no longer worthy to be called your son; make me like one of your hired men.' So he got up and went to his father.

"But while he was still a long way off, his father saw him and was filled with compassion for him; he ran to his son, threw his arms around him and kissed him. The son said to him, 'Father, I have sinned against heaven and against you. I am no longer worthy to be called your son.' But the father said to his servants, 'Quick! Bring the best robe and put it on him. Put a ring on his finger and sandals on his feet. Bring the fattened calf and kill it. Let's have a feast and celebrate. For this son of mine was dead and is alive again; he was lost and is found.' So they began to celebrate."

Luke 15:11-24

18

Like the younger son, we have been given: the robe – we have been restored to a position of "right standing" with God; the ring – we have incredible power and authority in Christ; and the sandals – we have become children of God Himself and have all the rights and privileges of children.

Chat

Can you identify yourself with the younger son in the story? If so, in what ways?

How does the father in the story change the way you think about God and your relationship with Him?

Which of the items given to the younger son (and therefore to you too) is most significant to you? Why? What difference will knowing this make to you day to day?

EXTRA
FILM

ON THE
APP

WHY
BELIEVE
THE BIBLE?

Outrageous choice

The older brother thought he could please his father by working hard and doing the right thing. He was angry when the father simply accepted his little brother back and didn't even punish him. He didn't realize that he was already pleasing to his father just because of who he was.

The point Jesus was making is that God does not love you because of the good things you do. Or stop loving you when you do terrible things. In fact it's not about what you do at all. He loves you for who you are.

Disciple:
someone who is learning to
become more and more like Jesus
in character, and who will
therefore behave more and more
like Him.

Reflect

At the end of every session, we encourage you to have a time of reflection. Consider questions such as the following: What has God shown you today? What points have particularly struck you? Have you become aware of any faulty thinking, anything you have believed that you now realize is not in line with what is actually true according to God? If so, write it down on the pages at the end of this book.

Making our life stories count is not about trying harder or striving to follow God. It's simply about knowing God and knowing who you are. It all flows from your God-given identity and relationship with Jesus. However, it's by no means inevitable that you'll leave an eternal legacy – and making the choice to do so goes right against the prevailing culture.

List some things that may be holding you back

There are things that want to hold you back and will do if you let them. But *disciple* will help you work out what they are and how to overcome them – every time.

Going deeper

In the "Going deeper" section, you will find suggestions for things you can work on at home in between sessions in order to take the truths deeper. The *disciple* app has some additional help on that.

The truths in this session can be absolutely life changing if you can really take hold of them in your heart.

• Read through Luke 15:11–24 (it's printed on page 18) and then take some time in quiet prayer to imagine the story again. Imagine yourself as the son or daughter returning, and God as the father. How does it make you feel to know that once you return to Him, you are loved completely and unconditionally, no matter what has happened to you or what you have done in your life?

• Think again about the ring, the robe, and the sandals and what they symbolize. Remind yourself that, if you're a Christian, you <u>already</u> have them. Spend some time with God making a choice to use them in your life.

• Read the rest of the story (Luke 15:25–32). Can you recognize anything of the older brother's attitude in you? In your relationship with God are you more like a son or a servant?

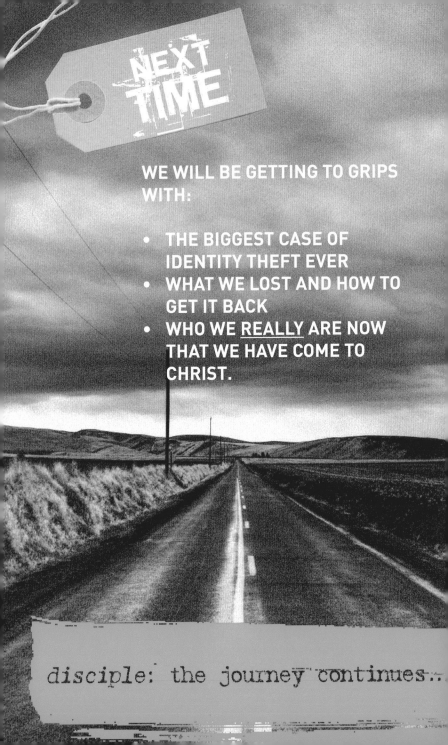

NEXT TIME

WE WILL BE GETTING TO GRIPS WITH:

- THE BIGGEST CASE OF IDENTITY THEFT EVER
- WHAT WE LOST AND HOW TO GET IT BACK
- WHO WE <u>REALLY</u> ARE NOW THAT WE HAVE COME TO CHRIST.

disciple: the journey continues...

How the story starts

> Paul, an apostle of Christ Jesus by the will of God;
> To God's holy people in Ephesus, the faithful in Christ Jesus.
>
> **Ephesians 1:1**

The disobedience of Adam and Eve left us spiritually dead with driving needs to be <u>significant</u>, <u>secure</u>, and <u>accepted</u>. Becoming Christians meant a huge change in our identity and story. We are no longer spiritual orphans but holy people who are spiritually alive! And all our needs are now met in Christ.

If you were introduced to someone you didn't know, what is the most surprising thing you could tell them about yourself, something you did, or something that happened to you?

What are some of the key things that give you a sense of your own unique identity? (They may perhaps be to do with your culture, your achievements, your role in life, or other things).

The problem:

So God created mankind in his own image, in the image of God he created them; male and female he created them.

Genesis 1:27

As for you, you were dead in your transgressions and sins.

Ephesians 2:1

We are more than we see – we are made in God's image which means that we are spiritual beings too.

At the fall Adam and Eve messed things up for us. It was a total catastrophe for humankind.

We are all now born spiritually dead with a driving need to find the significance, security, and acceptance that they lost.

Chat

disciple

What (if anything) do you know about your ancestors and your family tree?

Can you see ways of thinking and acting that have been passed down your family line? For example are there things that your ancestors were good at that you are too, or things that they struggled with that you do too?

How different do you think life would be if we had not been born spiritually dead but instead were born connected to God and were able to chat with Him as we are chatting to one another now?

2

The cure

- If you are a Christian you are now part of God's story and restored as His child.

- When we came to Christ we were reconnected to God and our spiritual life was restored.

- All Christians have become a brand new creation. We are holy ones (saints) – no matter what our back story is!

- The significance, security, and acceptance we were designed to have are fully restored to us in Jesus.

Astonishing truths about who you now are!

Yet to all who did receive him, to those who believed in his name, he gave the right to become children of God.
John 1:12

"I have come that they may have life, and have it to the full."
John 10:10

"Whoever has the Son has LIFE. Whoever does not have the Son of God does not have LIFE."
1 John 5:12

"I am the resurrection and the LIFE. He who believes in me will LIVE, even though they die."
John 11:25

Therefore, if anyone is in Christ, he is a new creation. The old has passed away; behold, the new has come.
2 Corinthians 5:17 (ESV)

God made him who had no sin to be sin for us, so that in him we might become the righteousness of God.
2 Corinthians 5:21

List other verses here as you go through disciple

Chat

How hard do you find it to believe that, since you are in Christ, you have become a holy one, a saint, without any effort on your part? Why?

What difference would it make to your life to know that, deep down, you are a delight to God just because of who you now are and that nothing and nobody can change that?

Will knowing this be more likely to make you think, "So I can live however I like" or "I really want to serve God, not because I have to but because I want to"? Why?

Whoever does not love does not know God, because God is love.

1 John 4:8

Therefore, there is now no condemnation for those who are in Christ Jesus.

Romans 8:1

My dear children, I write this to you so that you will not sin. But if anybody does sin, we have an advocate with the Father— Jesus Christ, the Righteous One.

1 John 2:1

God loves us no matter what we have done or what we do.

We may not feel significant, secure, and accepted but we need to start with what God says is true, not our feelings. What you believe about yourself will always work out in how you behave.

We do still go wrong. But when that happens, it doesn't change the fact that we are holy ones. We simply need to acknowledge our mistake, say sorry, and choose not to do it again.

Who we are
What we do

TRUTH
ENCOUNTER

Who I Am In Jesus

I renounce the lie that I am rejected, unloved, dirty, or shameful because in Jesus I am completely ACCEPTED. God says that:

I am God's child (see John 1:12)

I am Jesus' friend (see John 15:15)

I have been justified (see Romans 5:1)

I am united with God and I am one spirit with Him (see 1 Corinthians 6:17)

I have been bought with a price: I belong to God (see 1 Corinthians 6:19–20)

I am a member of Jesus' body (see 1 Corinthians 12:27)

I am a saint, a holy one (see Ephesians 1:1)

I have been adopted as God's child (see Ephesians 1:5)

I have direct access to God through the Holy Spirit (see Ephesians 2:18)

I am forgiven of all my sins (see Colossians 1:14)

I am complete in Jesus (see Colossians 2:10)

I renounce the lie that I am guilty, unprotected, alone, or abandoned because in Jesus I am totally SECURE. God says that:

I am free forever from condemnation (see Romans 8:1–2)

I am assured that all things work together for good (see Romans 8:28)

I am free from all condemning charges against me (see Romans 8:31–34)

I cannot be separated from the love of God (see Romans 8:35–39)

I have been established, anointed, and sealed by God (see 2 Corinthians 1:21–22)

I am confident that the good work God has begun in me will be perfected (see Philippians 1:6)

I am a citizen of heaven (see Philippians 3:20)

I am hidden with Jesus in God (see Colossians 3:3)

I have not been given a spirit of fear, but of power, love, and a sound mind (see 2 Timothy 1:7)

I can find grace and mercy to help me when I need it (see Hebrews 4:16)

I am born of God and the evil one cannot touch me (see 1 John 5:18)

I renounce the lie that I am worthless, inadequate, helpless, or hopeless because in Jesus I am deeply SIGNIFICANT. God says that:

I am the salt of the earth and the light of the world (see Matthew 5:13–14)

I am a branch of the true vine, Jesus, a channel of His life (see John 15:1–5)

I have been chosen and appointed by God to bear fruit (see John 15:16)

I am a personal, Spirit empowered witness of Jesus (see Acts 1:8)

I am a temple of God (see 1 Corinthians 3:16)

I am a minister of reconciliation for God (see 2 Corinthians 5:17–21)

I am God's fellow worker (see 2 Corinthians 6:1)

I am seated with Jesus in the heavenly realms (see Ephesians 2:6)

I am God's workmanship, created for good works (see Ephesians 2:10)

I can come to God with freedom and confidence (see Ephesians 3:12)

I can do all things through Jesus who strengthens me (see Philippians 4:13)

I am not the great "I Am", but by the grace of God I am what I am
(see Exodus 3:14; John 8:24, 28, 58; 1 Corinthians 15:10).

Reflect

Read through the "Who I Am In Jesus" list again.

Even better, get into twos and read the list slowly to your partner changing "I" to "you". So you would start by saying, "You are not rejected, unloved, dirty..." etc. and then "You are God's child"etc. Swap over when you have finished.

- Which truths stand out to you the most? Write them down or highlight them in your Bible.

- How does it make you feel to realize that Jesus paid with His life so that you could be reconnected to God and have an intimate relationship with him? Spend some time thanking God and telling Him how you feel.

When you realize that an area in your belief system is not in line with what God says is true, remember to write it down on pages 190–191 together with the corresponding truth.

Going deeper

In order to make sure you really get hold of these life-changing truths, find some time in the coming week to reflect on the following:

- Slowly read the "Who I Am In Jesus" list from this session out loud. Let each one sink in before moving on to the next one.

- Look up the Bible references alongside the items in the list.

- Do you accept that, if God says the things on the list are true of you, then they are true, no matter how you may feel?

- If you are struggling with this, why not take some quiet time with God and ask Him to show you how He sees you.

We recommend you continue to read the list out loud once or twice a day until you feel you have taken hold of who you really are in Jesus. It may take several weeks. You will find the list on the *disciple* app so why not use it whenever you have a spare moment?

NEXT TIME

WE WILL BE WORKING OUT:

- WHAT <u>TRUTH</u> IS AND WHETHER OR NOT IT IS TRUE FOR EVERYONE
- WHAT <u>FAITH</u> IS
- HOW WE CAN INCREASE OUR FAITH.

disciple: the journey continues..

03

A true story

WHY?

> Jesus answered, "You say that I am a king. In fact, the reason I was born and came into the world is to testify to the truth. Everyone on the side of truth listens to me."
> "What is truth?" retorted Pilate.
>
> **John 18:37-38**

"What is truth?" is a question that people have been asking for thousands of years.

Jesus didn't claim to know truth. He claimed actually to BE the truth.

Faith is simply making a choice to believe in Jesus as the truth rather than following feelings.

If you saw someone about to jump off a high wall because they had a sincerely-held belief that gravity wouldn't affect them, would you be prepared to disregard their belief and try to prevent them jumping? Or do you think there is a strong case for respecting their belief and not interfering? Why?

Tell the group about a time when you acted on false information, when you believed something that turned out not to be true.

Truth is true

"I am the way, and the truth, and the life; no one comes to the Father but through Me."

John 14:6 (NASB)

Our culture makes it hard for us to think that there can be one absolute and universal truth that applies to all people everywhere at all times.

But logic clearly demonstrates that this is the case. When we die, we'll all experience the same thing: either we'll all cease to exist, or we'll all stand before God, or we will all experience some other thing.

Believing something does not make it true and not believing something does not make it untrue. Truth is true regardless of what we choose to believe.

Chat

Is it important to you to find the truth? Why or why not?

Do you believe that there is such a thing as truth that is true for everyone at all times in all places? Why do you think this concept makes some people uncomfortable?

How does the statement that Jesus is the way, the truth and the life (John 14:6) make you feel? Why? How might you approach sharing this with others?

Faith is a choice

> Jesus Christ is the same yesterday and today and forever.
>
> **Hebrews 13:8**
>
> "If you have faith as small as a mustard seed, you can say to this mountain, 'Move from here to there,' and it will move. Nothing will be impossible for you."
>
> **Matthew 17:20**
>
> In the same way, faith by itself, if it is not accompanied by action, is dead. But someone will say, "You have faith; I have deeds." Show me your faith without deeds, and I will show you my faith by my deeds.
>
> **James 2:17-18**

Faith is simply making a choice to believe what God says is true. It's about bringing your belief system into line with what is already true.

The effectiveness of your faith is not determined by how strong it feels but by the strength and reliability of the one you put your faith in.

Growing in faith is about growing in relationship with God – as we get to know Him better, we'll trust Him more.

Faith:

Faith grows when you make a choice to believe what God says is true, stand firm on that, and step out into action.

Chat

disciple

How does the realization that faith is simply a choice
you make change the way you feel about God and
your daily life?

How could you get to know God better?

Would you like to take the opportunity to commit to
spending more time with God? Take a moment to ask
God to help you work out how best to make more time
to grow in your relationship with Him. Pray for one
another.

And we know that in all things God works for the good of those who love him, who have been called according to his purpose.

Romans 8:28 (ESV)

God will make good come even from our struggles.

When we learn to follow God rather than our feelings when times get tough, we will grow in our relationship with God.

"Never doubt in the dark what God told you in the light." Raymond Edman.

The Can Do List

1. Why should I say I can't do it when the Bible says I can do all things through Jesus who gives me strength (Philippians 4:13)?

2. Why should I lack when I know that God will supply all my needs according to His riches in glory in Jesus (Philippians 4:19)?

3. Why should I be afraid when the Bible says God has not given me a spirit of fear, but one of power, love, and a sound mind (2 Timothy 1:7)?

4. Why should I lack faith to complete my calling knowing that God has given me a measure of faith (Romans 12:3)?

5. Why should I be weak when the Bible says that God is the strength of my life and that I will be strong and take action because I know Him (Psalm 27:1; Daniel 11:32)?

6. Why should I allow Satan supremacy in my life when He that is in me is greater than he that is in the world (1 John 4:4)?

7. Why should I accept defeat when the Bible says that God always leads me in victory (2 Corinthians 2:14)?

8. Why should I be without wisdom when Christ became wisdom to me from God and God gives me wisdom generously when I ask Him for it (1 Corinthians 1:30; James 1:5)?

9. Why should I be depressed when I can remember God's loving kindness, compassion and faithfulness and have hope (Lamentations 3:21–23)?

10. Why should I worry when I can cast all my anxiety on Jesus who cares for me (1 Peter 5:7)?

11. Why should I ever be in bondage when I know that, where the Spirit of God is, there is freedom (2 Corinthians 3:17; Galatians 5:1)?

12. Why should I feel guilty when the Bible says I am not guilty because I am in Jesus (Romans 8:1)?

13. Why should I feel alone when Jesus said He is with me always and He will never leave me or let me go (Matthew 28:20; Hebrews 13:5)?

14. Why should I feel cursed or that I am the victim of bad luck when the Bible says that Jesus redeemed me from the curse of the law that I can receive His Spirit (Galatians 3:13–14)?

15. Why should I be discontent when, like Paul, I can learn to be content in all my circumstances (Philippians 4:11)?

16. Why should I feel worthless when Jesus became sin for me so that I could become the righteousness of God in Him (2 Corinthians 5:21)?

17. Why should I have a persecution complex knowing that nobody can be against me when God is for me (Romans 8:31)?

18. Why should I be confused when God is the author of peace and gives me knowledge through the Holy Spirit who lives in me (1 Corinthians 14:33; 1 Corinthians 2:12)?

19. Why should I feel like a failure when I am a conqueror in all things through Jesus (Romans 8:37)?

20. Why should I let the pressures of life bother me when I can take courage knowing that Jesus has overcome the world and its tribulations (John 16:33)?

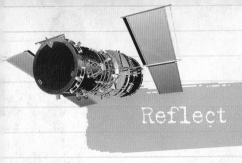

Reflect

Read "The Can Do List" out loud. Even better, find a partner and read it to each other changing "I" to "You".

Which three truths most stand out to you? Write them below. Share with each other why you have selected these particular ones.

Do you know someone who is really struggling at the moment? How could you come alongside them and show them that they are loved? Spend some time praying for them.

When you realize that an area in your belief system is not in line with what God says is true, remember to write it down on pages 190–191 together with the corresponding truth.

Going deeper

Read "The Can Do List" out loud slowly, letting each one sink in. Look up the corresponding verses in your Bible for the three that stand out to you the most. You could write the verses out and pin them up somewhere you will see them every day.

Life can be hard at times for all of us. If you have stuff that you're finding tough at the moment, tell God about it. See if He has anything to say to you about it.

If you're really struggling, seek out a Christian friend or pastor who can support you and pray with you.

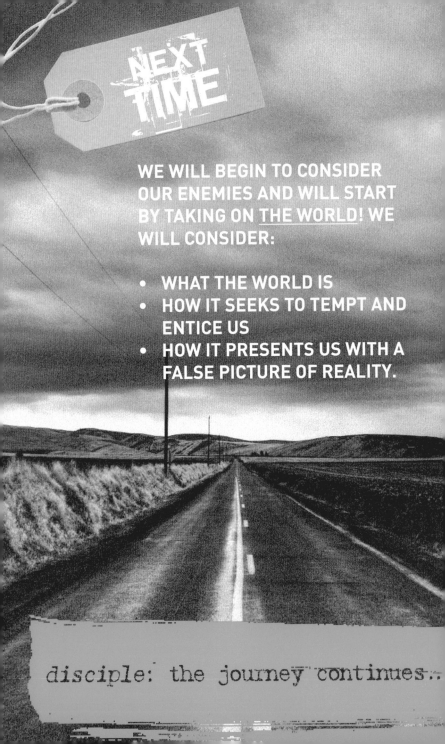

NEXT TIME

WE WILL BEGIN TO CONSIDER
OUR ENEMIES AND WILL START
BY TAKING ON <u>THE WORLD</u>! WE
WILL CONSIDER:

- WHAT THE WORLD IS
- HOW IT SEEKS TO TEMPT AND
  ENTICE US
- HOW IT PRESENTS US WITH A
  FALSE PICTURE OF REALITY.

disciple: the journey continues...

The story of the world

WHY?

Do not conform to the pattern of this world, but be transformed by the renewing of your mind. Then you will be able to test and approve what God's will is – his good, pleasing and perfect will.

Romans 12:2

The world seeks to knock us off track and redirect our life stories away from the plans that God has for us through false promises, consumerism, and comfort, and by presenting us with a false picture of reality.

How would you feel if you were deprived of the ability to go online or use your favourite media?

If you were in charge of marketing some new consumer product (maybe a clothing range, a new electronic gizmo, or a luxury foodstuff) what message would you put in your advertising to try to persuade people they need it?

False promises

"I do not ask that you take them out of the world, but that you keep them from the evil one. They are not of the world, just as I am not of the world. Sanctify them in the truth; your word is truth."

John 17:15-17 (ESV)

Satan is the ruler of the world (John 12:31, 14:30) and is behind its false promises to us.

The world promises to meet our needs for significance, acceptance and security and says:

- Perform well + Accomplish = Significance
- Status + Wealth = Security
- Good Image + Admiration = Acceptance

Seeking comfort and consumerism exert a huge subliminal pull on us.

The world's promises are bankrupt and count for nothing eternally.

Ctrl+C

DO NOT STORE UP FOR YOURSELVES TREASURES ON EARTH, WHERE MOTHS AND VERMIN DESTROY, AND WHERE THIEVES BREAK IN AND STEAL. BUT STORE UP FOR YOURSELVES TREASURES IN HEAVEN, WHERE MOTHS AND VERMIN DO NOT DESTROY, AND WHERE THIEVES DO NOT BREAK IN AND STEAL.

Matthew 6:19-20

Chat

How have you seen the world's false promises at play in life? How do these false promises shape the way society views someone who has nothing – a homeless person on the street for example?

Have you ever fallen for the idea that having the right "stuff" marks you out as having "made it" or being worth "knowing"? How? What can we do to counter this idea in our lives?

Which of the three false promises are you most vulnerable to? How can you combat it in your daily life?

Distractions and enticements

Do not love the world or anything in the world. If anyone loves the world, love for the Father is not in them. For everything in the world – the lust of the flesh, the lust of the eyes and the pride of life – comes not from the Father but from the world. The world and its desires pass away, but whoever does the will of God lives forever.

1 John 2:15–17

The lust of the flesh, the lust of the eyes, and the pride of life seek to entice us but lead to nothing but darkness and bondage.

Lust of the flesh = the pull on our bodies to form unhelpful habits like comfort eating and sleeping around.

Lust of the eyes = when we lose ourselves in screens looking at pornography, horror, or celebrities.

Pride of life = the pull on our egos to achieve and boast.

DO YOU NOT KNOW THAT HE WHO IS
JOINED TO A PROSTITUTE BECOMES
ONE BODY WITH HER? FOR, AS IT IS
WRITTEN, "THE TWO WILL BECOME
ONE FLESH."

1 Corinthians 6:16

"THE EYE IS THE LAMP OF THE
BODY. IF YOUR EYES ARE HEALTHY,
YOUR WHOLE BODY WILL BE FULL
OF LIGHT. BUT IF YOUR EYES ARE
UNHEALTHY, YOUR WHOLE BODY
WILL BE FULL OF DARKNESS."

Matthew 6:22-23

BUT HE GIVES US MORE GRACE.
THAT IS WHY SCRIPTURE SAYS:
"GOD OPPOSES THE PROUD BUT
SHOWS FAVOUR TO THE HUMBLE."

James 4:6

Chat

"Sex is a beautiful gift from God when it is enjoyed in the way He intended?" Do you agree with this statement? Why or why not? (Note: if you want to know more about this, when you get home you can watch an extra teaching film on it via the app).

How do you feel about the idea that what you look at can affect your spiritual health? What practical things could you do to protect your spiritual health with regard to this?

"Though the LORD is great, he cares for the humble, but he keeps his distance from the proud." (Psalm 138:6, NLT). Why do you think pride is so abhorrent to God?

False reality

> "I am the way, and the truth, and the life; no one comes to the Father but through Me."
>
> **John 14:6 (NASB)**
>
> Do not conform to the pattern of this world, but be transformed by the renewing of your mind.
>
> **Romans 12:2**

We all inherit from our culture a way of making sense of reality but our worldview paints a false picture of reality.

God tells us in the Bible what reality is actually like. When we adopt the "biblical worldview" we will see the world as it really is.

We need to critically evaluate the views that we have absorbed from our culture and environment to make sure that we do not have a "salad bar" or "pick 'n' mix" faith.

Reflect

It can be very difficult to realize that we have a worldview. Use this time to help each other grasp this by considering these questions:

- If you had been born thirty years earlier, how would the way you look at the world have been different? If you had been born thirty years later, do you think it would be different again?

- If you had been born in a different culture, how might the way you see life be different?

- What does this tell you about whether or not your worldview is accurately representing reality?

- Are you able to identify areas where you have taken a "salad bar" or "pick 'n' mix" approach to faith, that is, where you have chosen to overlook some things that God says in His Word?

When you realize that an area in your belief system is not in line with what God says is true, remember to write it down on pages 190–191 together with the corresponding truth.

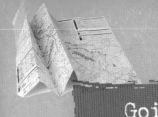

Going deeper

Remember, the battle we are in takes place in our minds and is a battle between truth and lies. Start by saying a prayer to dedicate yourself to seeing reality as God says it is.

Have you realized that you have been trusting your traditional worldview more than God's Word? If so, spend some time in prayer rejecting your worldview and committing yourself to the Biblical worldview.

Ask God to show you what things in the world entice you most effectively. Consider how you can make it less likely that you will fall for their deception.

EXTRA FILM

ON THE APP

THE GIFT OF SEX

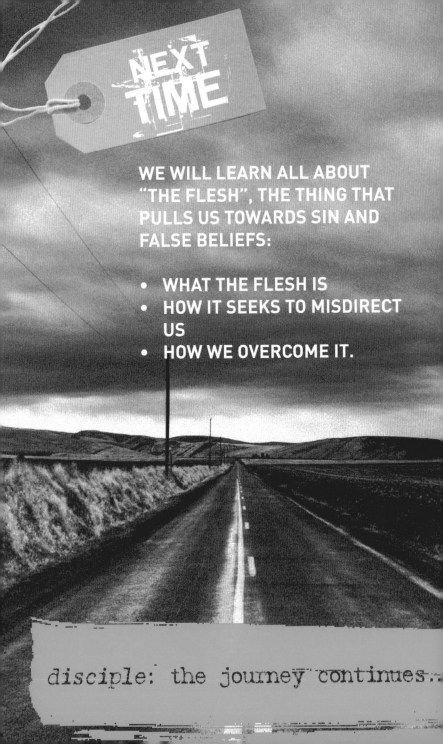

NEXT TIME

WE WILL LEARN ALL ABOUT "THE FLESH", THE THING THAT PULLS US TOWARDS SIN AND FALSE BELIEFS:

- WHAT THE FLESH IS
- HOW IT SEEKS TO MISDIRECT US
- HOW WE OVERCOME IT.

disciple: the journey continues...

05

The story of
the flesh

WHY?

You, however, are not in the flesh but in the Spirit, if in fact the Spirit of God dwells in you.

Romans 8:9 (ESV)

The weapons we fight with are not the weapons of the world. On the contrary, they have divine power to demolish strongholds.

2 Corinthians 10:4

The flesh is what comes naturally to a fallen human being. It consists of beliefs and thoughts that are contrary to God's truth that pull us towards sin and hopelessness.

Although we became new creations and holy ones when we turned to Jesus, no one pressed a "delete" button in our minds. Those unhelpful ways of thinking are still there. We do, however, have everything we need to overcome the flesh. But it requires some effort and persistence.

Which people from your past have had the most positive influence on who you are today?

What people or experiences from your past have had the most negative impact on how you see yourself?

Understanding the flesh

> Those who live according to the flesh have their minds set on what the flesh desires; but those who live in accordance with the Spirit have their minds set on what the Spirit desires. The mind governed by the flesh is death, but the mind governed by the Spirit is life and peace.
>
> **Romans 8:5-7**

Christianity is not a quick-fix. Becoming like Jesus is a process that takes time and effort. We need to be intentional about becoming a fruitful disciple.

When we became Christians we changed but the pull of the flesh didn't disappear.

Being a disciple is not about everything in life being easy and feeling good. It's about a relationship with God who promises to help you through whatever life throws at you and make your life count for eternity.

Chat

disciple

If the flesh is "what comes naturally to a fallen human" or "default programming", can you think of some of the ways it shows up in your life or in other people's lives?

Where do you tend to look for comfort when life is tough or things go wrong?

Do you recognize in your own life or in other people's lives the tendency to believe the lie that says "the goal of being a Christian is to feel good and be happy"? What are the dangers of falling for this lie?

Natural, spiritual or fleshly?

Through Christ Jesus the law of the Spirit who gives life has set you free from the law of sin and death.

Romans 8:2

So I say, walk by the Spirit, and you will not gratify the desires of the flesh.

Galatians 5:16

His divine power has given us everything we need for a godly life through our knowledge of him who called us by his own glory and goodness.

2 Peter 1:3

Paul categorizes all people into three types:
- The natural person is a not-yet-Christian, someone who is spiritually dead.
- The spiritual person lives by the Spirit and crucifies their flesh daily (see Galatians 5:22–23).
- The fleshly person is a Christian who is living in contradiction to their new identity in Christ and whose life looks more like that of a not-yet-Christian.

Living as a spiritual person is perfectly possible, indeed it should be our expectation. But we can be held back by:
- Not knowing the truth
- Deception
- Unresolved personal or spiritual issues.

"The law of sin and death" is still in force and pulls us towards sin but we can choose to overcome it by a greater law – the law of the Spirit of life!

THE **NATURAL PERSON** DOES NOT ACCEPT THE THINGS OF THE SPIRIT OF GOD, FOR THEY ARE FOLLY TO HIM, AND HE IS NOT ABLE TO UNDERSTAND THEM BECAUSE THEY ARE SPIRITUALLY DISCERNED. THE **SPIRITUAL PERSON** JUDGES ALL THINGS, BUT IS HIMSELF TO BE JUDGED BY NO ONE. "FOR WHO HAS UNDERSTOOD THE MIND OF THE LORD SO AS TO INSTRUCT HIM?" BUT WE HAVE THE MIND OF CHRIST.

BUT I, BROTHERS, COULD NOT ADDRESS YOU AS SPIRITUAL PEOPLE, BUT AS **PEOPLE OF THE FLESH**, AS INFANTS IN CHRIST. I FED YOU WITH MILK, NOT SOLID FOOD, FOR YOU WERE NOT READY FOR IT. AND EVEN NOW YOU ARE NOT YET READY, FOR YOU ARE STILL OF THE FLESH. FOR WHILE THERE IS JEALOUSY AND STRIFE AMONG YOU, ARE YOU NOT OF THE FLESH AND BEHAVING ONLY IN A HUMAN WAY?

1 Corinthians 2:14 – 3:3 (ESV)

Chat

disciple

Look at 1 Corinthians 2:14–3:3 (on page 81). Which type of person would you say you are: a natural person (does not yet know Jesus); a spiritual person (knows Jesus and walks by the Spirit); or a fleshly person (knows Jesus but walks by the flesh)?

Which type of person would you like to be?

Do you agree that living as a spiritual person is not some unattainable ideal but perfectly possible for every Christian? Why or why not?

3

Living by the Spirit

"Come to me, all you who are weary and burdened, and I will give you rest. Take my yoke upon you and learn from me, for I am gentle and humble in heart, and you will find rest for your souls."

Matthew 11:28-29

The fruit of the Spirit is love, joy, peace, forbearance, kindness, goodness, faithfulness, gentleness and self-control.

Galatians 5:22-23

No temptation has overtaken you except what is common to mankind. And God is faithful; he will not let you be tempted beyond what you can bear. But when you are tempted, he will also provide a way out so that you can endure it.

1 Corinthians 10:13

Living by the Spirit is a choice we make which is born out of our relationship with God.

If we continue to make good choices, we will automatically bear fruit. The fruit of the Spirit is all to do with our character.

All temptation is simply an attempt to get you to meet your legitimate needs for significance, security, and acceptance independently of God. There is always a way of escape and it comes right at the start of the thought process.

Reflect

What most struck you about what living by the Spirit really is and why?

What, if anything, is holding you back from maturing into the fruitful disciple God has created you to be?

Pray for each other. Why not take this opportunity to make a commitment to God and yourself to see this course through to the end?

When you realize that an area in your belief system is not in line with what God says is true, remember to write it down on pages 190–191 together with the corresponding truth.

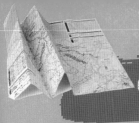

Going deeper

What temptations do you particularly struggle with?

Ask God to help you identify the thought processes that have led to you giving in to them in the past.

What would it look like to "take those thoughts captive" right at the start of the process?

Read Galatians 5:22–23 and think about those character attributes. Can you envisage them growing in your life as you continue to make good choices? How different would your life be if that happened?

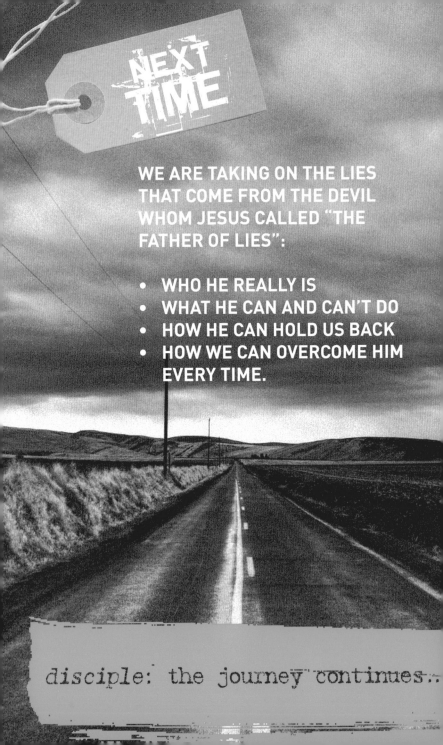

NEXT TIME

WE ARE TAKING ON THE LIES
THAT COME FROM THE DEVIL
WHOM JESUS CALLED "THE
FATHER OF LIES":

- WHO HE REALLY IS
- WHAT HE CAN AND CAN'T DO
- HOW HE CAN HOLD US BACK
- HOW WE CAN OVERCOME HIM
  EVERY TIME.

disciple: the journey continues...

The story of the devil

WHY?

Be alert and of sober mind. Your enemy the devil prowls around like a roaring lion looking for someone to devour. Resist him, standing firm in the faith, because you know that the family of believers throughout the world is undergoing the same kind of sufferings.

1 Peter 5:8–9

The devil is real but is a defeated foe. We already have everything we need to overcome him in our lives so that we can fulfil the amazing plans that God has for us and make our lives count. But to overcome him we need to understand who he is and how he works.

Declaration

In Jesus' name we declare that God is sovereign. We submit ourselves to God and tell every enemy of the Lord Jesus Christ to leave this place now. We declare that they cannot stop the will of God being done in this group or in our lives. We belong to Jesus and the evil one cannot touch us.

If you felt you weren't making enough progress in your walk with God and wanted to fix this, where might be a good place to start?

C. S. Lewis wrote, "There are two equal and opposite errors into which our race can fall about the devils. One is to disbelieve in their existence. The other is to believe, and to feel an excessive and unhealthy interest in them. They themselves are equally pleased by both errors, and hail a materialist or magician with the same delight." (C.S. Lewis, *The Screwtape Letters*, 1941, p. 3). Which of these two errors do you tend towards?

The devil and you

Now is the time for judgment on this world; now the prince
of this world will be driven out.

John 12:31

As for you, you were dead in your transgressions and sins,
in which you used to live when you followed the ways of this
world and of the ruler of the kingdom of the air, the spirit
who is now at work in those who are disobedient.

Ephesians 2:1-2

We know that we are children of God, and that the whole
world is under the control of the evil one.

1 John 5:19

The one who does what is sinful is of the devil, because the
devil has been sinning from the beginning. The reason the
Son of God appeared was to destroy the devil's work.

1 John 3:8

And having disarmed the powers and authorities, he made a
public spectacle of them, triumphing over them by the cross.

Colossians 2:15

Then Jesus came to them and said, "All authority in heaven
and on earth has been given to me. Therefore go and make
disciples of all nations, baptizing them in the name of the
Father and of the Son and of the Holy Spirit, and teaching
them to obey everything I have commanded you. And surely
I am with you always, to the very end of the age."

Matthew 28:18-20

And God raised us up with Christ and seated us with him in
the heavenly realms in Christ Jesus.

Ephesians 2:6

The one who was born of God keeps them safe, and the evil
one cannot harm them.

1 John 5:18

Lies, lies, lies...

> [The devil] was a murderer from the beginning, not holding to the truth, for there is no truth in him. When he lies, he speaks his native language, for he is a liar and the father of lies.
>
> **John 8:44**

Lie 1: He isn't real.

Lie 2: He is equal in power to God.

Lie 3: He is more powerful than we are.

Lie 4: We are immune to his tactics.

The truth is:
- Satan can do nothing to change our true identity as holy ones in Jesus Christ.
- We have much more power and authority than Satan does.
- Satan is already defeated.
- Satan's powers are NO match for God.

Satan has no power over us other than what we give him.

Chat

How hard do you find it to believe that the devil and demons are real? Why do you think that is?

Which of the four lies we looked at are you most susceptible to? What can you do about this?

Read Ephesians 6:11–18 (on the next page). What do you think it means in practice to put on the armour of God?

Put on the full armour of God, so that you can take your stand against the devil's schemes. For our struggle is not against flesh and blood, but against the rulers, against the authorities, against the powers of this dark world and against the spiritual forces of evil in the heavenly realms. Therefore put on the full armour of God, so that when the day of evil comes, you may be able to stand your ground, and after you have done everything, to stand. Stand firm then, with the belt of truth buckled around your waist, with the breastplate of righteousness in place, and with your feet fitted with the readiness that comes from the gospel of peace. In addition to all this, take up the shield of faith, with which you can extinguish all the flaming arrows of the evil one. Take the helmet of salvation and the sword of the Spirit, which is the word of God. And pray in the Spirit on all occasions with all kinds of prayers and requests. With this in mind, be alert and always keep on praying for all the Lord's people.

Ephesians 6:11–18

2

The devil's tactics

"In your anger do not sin": Do not let the sun go down while you are still angry, and do not give the devil a foothold.
Ephesians 4:26–27

Submit yourselves, then, to God. Resist the devil, and he will flee from you.
James 4:7

The Spirit clearly says that in later times some will abandon the faith and follow deceiving spirits and things taught by demons.
1 Timothy 4:1

Satan has only three tactics: to tempt, to accuse, and to deceive.

Temptation
Remember, temptation is an attempt to get you to meet your legitimate need for significance, security, and acceptance outside of God.

If we fall for temptation we give the devil a foothold.

Although a Christian can allow the enemy some influence in their life through sin they can never become completely taken over ("possessed") by demons. At our very core is the Holy Spirit. We belong to God and Satan can never take us back.

Accusation

This comes once we've succumbed to temptation – like a double punch.

We need to know that there really is no condemnation for us, at least not from God, the only one who matters! (See Romans 8:1).

Deception

By definition, we don't know when we are being deceived.

Our greatest weapon is knowing the truth of God's word.

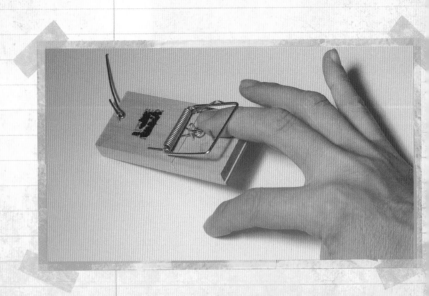

Footholds:

We give the devil footholds through sin. The way to resolve them is to submit to God through repentance and then resist him. At that point he has to FLEE from us. See James 4:7.

Chat

Does it surprise you to learn that not every thought that comes into your mind is your own? Is it more important to work out where a thought is coming from or to test it to see whether or not it is true?

Read Ephesians 4:26–27. What do you think the effects of giving the devil a foothold in your life would actually look like in everyday life?

If you are being deceived, by definition you don't know it. Share some examples of ways you have been deceived by the enemy in the past. How can you uncover ways he may be deceiving you right now?

Stand firm!

I will build my church, and the gates of hell shall not prevail against it.

Matthew 16:18b (ESV)

Our defence is knowing the truth of God's word and putting on the armour of God.

We have no reason to fear the devil, or go on demon hunts.

We need to know about the devil and demons and how they work so that we can take the necessary precautions. But we don't need to focus on them – we focus on Jesus and living a righteous life.

We are not called to drive out the darkness – we are called to turn on the light!

Reflect

Deception is Satan's most effective tactic because if you are being deceived, by definition you don't know about it!

Do you think it is possible that you are being deceived right now?

Pray for each other in pairs – that the Holy Spirit would lead you into all truth, especially as you prepare to go through *The Steps To Freedom In Christ* soon where you will be able to deal with the things that are holding you back.

When you realize that an area in your belief system is not in line with what God says is true, remember to write it down on pages 190–191 together with the corresponding truth.

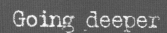

Going deeper

How does the enemy tend to tempt you?

How does he tend to accuse you?

If you are struggling to work these out, ask God to show you.

What will you do next time the tempting or accusing thoughts come? Are there any Bible verses that would be helpful for you to remember? You could write them out and pin them up somewhere to remind you.

EXTRA FILM

ON THE APP

THE TRUTH BEHIND THE OCCULT

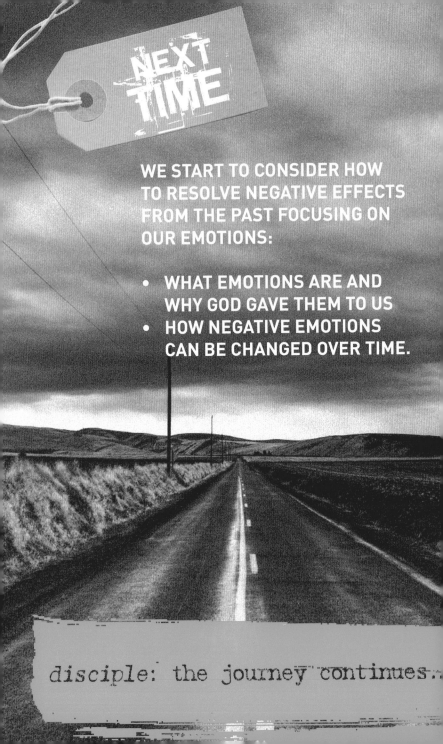

NEXT TIME

WE START TO CONSIDER HOW
TO RESOLVE NEGATIVE EFFECTS
FROM THE PAST FOCUSING ON
OUR EMOTIONS:

- WHAT EMOTIONS ARE AND
  WHY GOD GAVE THEM TO US
- HOW NEGATIVE EMOTIONS
  CAN BE CHANGED OVER TIME.

disciple: the journey continues...

Truth and emotions

"In your anger do not sin": do not let the sun go down while you are still angry, and do not give the devil a foothold."

Ephesians 4:26-27

Cast all your anxiety on him because he cares for you. Be alert and of sober mind. Your enemy the devil prowls around like a roaring lion looking for someone to devour.

1 Peter 5:7-8

Note the link between emotions (anger and anxiety) and giving ground in our lives to the devil in the now-familiar passages above.

Our emotions are given to us by God and serve as barometers of our spiritual health. It's essential to heed what they tell us and make adjustments when necessary if we want to stay on track.

Declaration

In Jesus' name we declare that God is sovereign in this place and over our lives and we submit ourselves to Him. We declare that we are here by legal right and that every enemy of the Lord Jesus Christ must be silent and leave this place immediately.

Have your emotions ever run away with you? Or has there ever been a time when you wished you could have let your emotions run away with you a little more than you did? What happened?

Do you think, on balance, that our emotions are a good thing or a bad thing? Why? If you agree that they were given to us by God, what purpose do you think He had in mind for them?

What are our emotions?

> "I will never leave you nor forsake you."
> **Hebrews 13:5 (ESV)**

Emotions are given to us by God as a gift for our own good but it's easy to trust them rather than the truth in God's Word.

Emotions act as signposts to what is happening in our soul. Negative emotions are to your inner person what the ability to feel physical pain is to your body.

When we feel angry, anxious, or depressed, it may be a sign that something in our belief system is not right and that we have some adjustments to make.

Depression

In case you're wondering and just to be absolutely clear, we are not saying that <u>all</u> depression comes from faulty beliefs or goals that feel unreachable (see page 152). It can also be caused by biochemical issues. However, if you suffer from depression, we'd certainly recommend looking at your beliefs and goals before God to make sure that they are not a contributory factor.

Chat

disciple

Our generation stands accused of believing that the most important goal in life is personal happiness. In what ways do you recognize this in your own life or in the lives of those around you?

What are the dangers of making choices based on our feelings?

Having listened to what Rob has said, have you changed your opinion about whether your emotions are a good thing or a bad thing? Why or why not?

2

Can we change the way we feel?

> When Saul and all Israel heard these words of the Philistine, they were dismayed and greatly afraid.
>
> **1 Samuel 17:11 (ESV)**
>
> "The Lord who delivered me from the paw of the lion and from the paw of the bear will deliver me from the hand of this Philistine."
>
> **1 Samuel 17:37 (ESV)**

We can learn to manage our emotions but it takes time.

If what we believe doesn't reflect truth, our feelings won't reflect reality.

Life events don't determine how you feel but your perception of them does.

We are tempted to suppress our emotions or express them indiscriminately but God wants us to be emotionally real and honest (as David was in the prayer on page 112).

By making a choice to believe God's truth rather than our emotions, we'll find that our emotions will (eventually) line up with what's really true.

What on earth is this doing in the Bible?

Appoint someone evil to oppose my enemy; let an accuser stand at his right hand. When he is tried, let him be found guilty, and may his prayers condemn him. May his days be few; may another take his place of leadership. May his children be fatherless and his wife a widow. May his children be wandering beggars; may they be driven from their ruined homes. May a creditor seize all he has; may strangers plunder the fruits of his labour. May no one extend kindness to him or take pity on his fatherless children. May his descendants be cut off, their names blotted out from the next generation. May the iniquity of his fathers be remembered before the LORD; may the sin of his mother never be blotted out. May their sins always remain before the LORD, that he may blot out their name from the earth.

Psalm 109:6–15

Have you ever felt like that? Have you ever prayed like that?
Would it be right to pray like that?
Was God surprised or did He already know David felt this way?
Is He big enough to take a bit of a temper tantrum from us?
Why did He inspire David to write it down and put it in the Bible?

Chat

Talk about a time when your wrong perception of a situation caused you to get into an unnecessary emotional state.

What "Goliaths" do you have to face? How much bigger than your Goliaths is God? What can you do to ensure you see the situation as it really is?

Have a look at the passage from the Psalms on the previous page and discuss the questions below it.

3

Roots

Hear me, Lord, and answer me, for I am poor and needy. Guard my life, for I am faithful to you; save your servant who trusts in you. You are my God; have mercy on me, Lord, for I call to you all day long. Bring joy to your servant, Lord, for I put my trust in you.

Psalm 86:1-4

The negative emotions that plague us today often have their roots in our past. But it's not so much what happened to us in the past that's the problem – it's the lies we believe as a result of what happened.

What we feel and how we behave are dictated by what we REALLY believe in our hearts.

As children of God, we are not a product of our past. We are a product of Jesus' past – His life, death, resurrection, and ascension.

We don't feel our way into good behaviour – we behave our way into good feelings.

No one has a backstory too messed up to find their complete freedom and make their life count.

Reflect

- What struck you most in this session?

- What emotions do you most struggle with?

- What unhelpful way do you most tend to respond to your own emotions; ignore them, or explode?

- How does it make you feel to think that your past doesn't have to hold you back any more?

Spend some time praying for each other.

When you realize that an area in your belief system is not in line with what God says is true, remember to write it down on pages 190–191 together with the corresponding truth.

Going deeper

Many people have stuff in their past that they don't want to think about again. But walking in freedom means looking at it again with the comforting Holy Spirit so that you can recognize the lies you have come to believe and take steps to believe the truth instead. Remember, life's events don't determine how you feel but your perception of them does.

- Is there something in your past that you have been trying to hide from? Bring it to God in prayer. Ask God to show you what it caused you to believe about yourself or Him that may not actually be true. And ask Him to lead you into freedom from it once and for all as you continue through the course.

- If you are struggling with difficult emotions at the moment, tell God exactly how you're feeling, and ask Him to help you. It may be helpful to find a Christian friend or church leader who can help you if you're really struggling.

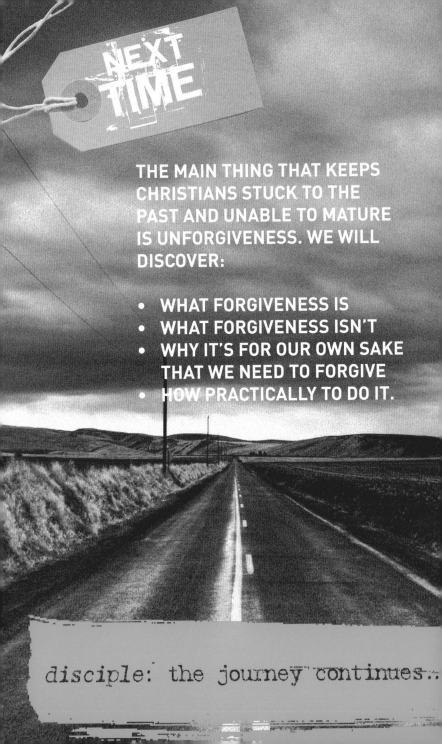

THE MAIN THING THAT KEEPS
CHRISTIANS STUCK TO THE
PAST AND UNABLE TO MATURE
IS UNFORGIVENESS. WE WILL
DISCOVER:

- WHAT FORGIVENESS IS
- WHAT FORGIVENESS ISN'T
- WHY IT'S FOR OUR OWN SAKE
  THAT WE NEED TO FORGIVE
- HOW PRACTICALLY TO DO IT.

disciple: the journey continues...

08

Forgiving from the heart

WHY?

"'Shouldn't you have had mercy on your fellow servant just as I had on you?' In anger his master handed him over to the jailers to be tortured, until he should pay back all he owed. This is how my heavenly Father will treat each of you unless you forgive your brother or sister from your heart."

Matthew 18:33-35

Most of us have not been taught what forgiveness really is and that it is for our own spiritual wellbeing that God commands us to forgive.

Declaration

I declare that my mind is my own and is to be a quiet place just for me and Jesus. I submit myself to God and I command – I don't suggest – I command every enemy of the Lord Jesus Christ to leave my presence immediately.

What other examples do you know where someone has exhibited radical forgiveness?

Do you think you could forgive someone completely for something as serious as Tamsin described in the film? Why or why not?

1

Why should I?

Be merciful, just as your Father is merciful.

Luke 6:36

Forgive us our sins, for we also forgive everyone who sins against us.

Luke 11:4

Anyone you forgive, I also forgive. And what I have forgiven – if there was anything to forgive – I have forgiven in the sight of Christ for your sake, in order that Satan might not outwit us. For we are not unaware of his schemes.

2 Corinthians 2:10–11

We forgive because God forgave us and because He commands us to do the same.

As we have seen, unforgiveness allows the devil a foothold (a place of influence) in our lives and can allow him to outwit us.

When we don't forgive, even though we ourselves have been forgiven, we become just like the unforgiving servant in Jesus' story and can suffer spiritual torment as a consequence.

The unforgiving servant

"Therefore, the kingdom of heaven is like a king who wanted to settle accounts with his servants. As he began the settlement, a man who owed him ten thousand talents was brought to him. Since he was not able to pay, the master ordered that he and his wife and his children and all that he had be sold to repay the debt.

"At this the servant fell on his knees before him. 'Be patient with me,' he begged, 'and I will pay back everything.' The servant's master took pity on him, cancelled the debt and let him go.

"But when that servant went out, he found one of his fellow servants who owed him a hundred silver coins. He grabbed him and began to choke him. 'Pay back what you owe me!' he demanded.

"His fellow servant fell to his knees and begged him, 'Be patient with me, and I will pay it back.'

"But he refused. Instead, he went off and had the man thrown into prison until he could pay the debt. When the other servants saw what had happened, they were outraged and went and told their master everything that had happened.

"Then the master called the servant in. 'You wicked servant,' he said, 'I cancelled all that debt of yours because you begged me to. Shouldn't you have had mercy on your fellow servant just as I had on you?' In anger his master handed him over to the jailers to be tortured, until he should pay back all he owed.

"This is how my heavenly Father will treat each of you unless you forgive your brother or sister from your heart."

Matthew 18:23-35

JUSTICE: Giving you what you deserve.

MERCY: Not giving you what you deserve.

GRACE: Giving you what you don't deserve.

Chat

How much have you been forgiven by God through Jesus? How might knowing this help you to forgive others?

How does God square the circle of the requirement for justice for all sins? To put it another way, how is God able to forgive us even though His righteous character demands that the debt of our sin is repaid?

2

What is forgiveness?

Submit yourselves for the Lord's sake to every human authority: whether to the emperor, as the supreme authority, or to governors, who are sent by him to punish those who do wrong and to commend those who do right.

1 Peter 2:13–14

Do not take revenge, my dear friends, but leave room for God's wrath, for it is written: "It is mine to avenge; I will repay," says the Lord.

Romans 12:19

Forgiveness is not forgetting what happened or saying it was OK.

Neither is it tolerating continual sin: you can forgive someone and still report them to the authorities if what they have done is illegal.

Forgiveness is not seeking revenge. It is taking a step of faith to hand it all over to God and trusting Him to make things right on our behalf. It means believing Him when He says, "I will repay". We make a choice to leave it in His hands so that we can walk away in freedom, no longer needing to seek revenge.

Chat

disciple

So, forgiveness is not forgetting, it's not tolerating sin, and it's not seeking revenge. How will knowing this help you to forgive those who have hurt you?

Does it surprise you that God promises you justice? How does this make it possible to forgive the people who have hurt us?

In the story we looked at in the first section, Jesus said we have to "forgive from the heart". What do you think that would look like in practice?

3

How do I do it?

If it is possible, as far as it depends on you, live at peace with everyone.

Romans 12:18

We have to be intentional about forgiving. We will never feel like forgiving – it's a choice we make in order to take hold of our freedom and heal our damaged emotions.

Forgiveness is an issue between us and God – you don't have to go to the person who hurt you.

Forgiveness doesn't mean you will necessarily be friends again afterwards – that does not depend entirely on you.

Forgiving means living with the consequences of their sin. But you are going to have to do that anyway. Your choice is whether to do it in the bondage of bitterness or the freedom of forgiveness.

Forgiving from the heart:

"God, I choose to forgive _____ for _____ which made me feel _____."

My Father God...

I renounce the lie that my Father God is distant or not interested in me.

I joyfully accept the truth that my Father God is intimate and involved (see Psalm 139:1–18).

I renounce the lie that my Father God is insensitive and uncaring.

I joyfully accept the truth that my Father God is kind and compassionate (see Psalm 103:8–14).

I renounce the lie that my Father God is strict and demanding.

I joyfully accept the truth that my Father God is accepting and filled with joy and love (see Romans 15:7; Zephaniah 3:17).

I renounce the lie that my Father God is passive and cold.

I joyfully accept the truth that my Father God is warm and affectionate (see Isaiah 40:11; Hosea 11:3–4).

I renounce the lie that my Father God is absent or too busy for me.

I joyfully accept the truth that my Father God is always with me and eager to be with me (see Hebrews 13:5; Jeremiah 31:20; Ezekiel 34:11–16).

I renounce the lie that my Father God is impatient, angry, or never satisfied with what I do.

I joyfully accept the truth that my Father God is patient and slow to anger and delights in those who put their hope in His unfailing love (see Exodus 34:6; 2 Peter 3:9; Psalm 147:11).

I renounce the lie that my Father God is mean, cruel, or abusive.

I joyfully accept the truth that my Father God loves me and is gentle and protective (see Jeremiah 31:3; Isaiah 42:3; Psalm 18:2).

I renounce the lie that my Father God is trying to take all the fun out of life.

I joyfully accept the truth that my Father God is trustworthy and wants to give me a full life; His will is good, perfect, and acceptable for me (see Lamentations 3:22–23; John 10:10; Romans 12:1–2).

I renounce the lie that my Father God is controlling or manipulative.

I joyfully accept the truth that my Father God is full of grace and mercy, and gives me freedom to fail (see Hebrews 4:15–16; Luke 15:11–16).

I renounce the lie that my Father God is condemning or unforgiving.

I joyfully accept the truth that my Father God is tender-hearted and forgiving; His heart and arms are always open to me (see Psalm 130:1–4; Luke 15:17–24).

I renounce the lie that my Father God is nit-picking or a demanding perfectionist.

I joyfully accept the truth that my Father God is committed to my growth and proud of me as His growing child (see Romans 8:28–29; Hebrews 12:5–11; 2 Corinthians 7:14).

I am the apple of His eye! (Deuteronomy 32:9–10).

EXTRA FILM   ON THE APP   GOD, MY FATHER

Reflect

Read through the "My Father God" truths again slowly.

Which truth strikes you the most? Why?

How do you feel as you approach *The Steps To Freedom In Christ* session (see page opposite)? Pray for each other in the light of that.

Going deeper

Invite the Holy Spirit to help you as you take a moment to consider the worst thing you have ever done. Take as long as you need to understand in your heart (not just your head) that God has completely and utterly forgiven you because of Jesus' death for you.

Ask God to show you someone you need to forgive and pledge to forgive them and anyone else you need to when you go through *The Steps To Freedom In Christ*.

In preparation for the Steps, meditate on Hebrews 12:1–2.

The Steps To Freedom
In Christ

Before the next session, you will have an opportunity to do business with God using *The Steps To Freedom In Christ*.

This is an amazing opportunity for you to have time with God and take hold of your freedom from personal and spiritual issues that are holding you back. You will have time to look at where you are being deceived, uncover lies you may believe, and deal with the rubbish you have picked up in your life story.

It's not some kind of group therapy session where you all hang your dirty washing out in front of each other – you will do your business on your own with God in a quiet place.

Remember to look out for lies (false beliefs) that come to light and write them down on pages 190–191.

It really is a great opportunity. Don't miss it!

EXTRA FILM

ON THE APP

INTRODUCTION TO THE STEPS TO FREEDOM IN CHRIST

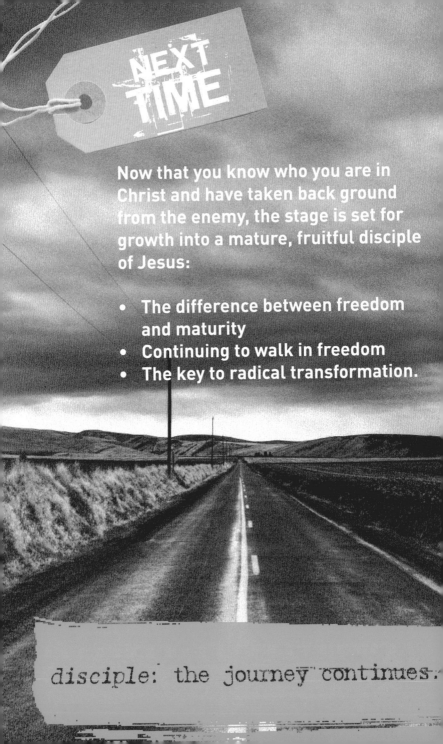

NEXT
TIME

Now that you know who you are in Christ and have taken back ground from the enemy, the stage is set for growth into a mature, fruitful disciple of Jesus:

- The difference between freedom and maturity
- Continuing to walk in freedom
- The key to radical transformation.

disciple: the journey continues.

09

Walking into the next chapter

WHY?

For though by this time you ought to be teachers, you need someone to teach you again the basic principles of the oracles of God. You need milk, not solid food, for everyone who lives on milk is unskilled in the word of righteousness, since he is a child. But solid food is for the mature, for those who have their powers of discernment trained by constant practice to distinguish good from evil.

Hebrews 5:12-14 (ESV)

Freedom is not the same thing as maturity but you can't mature until you have taken hold of your freedom. Are you now ready for solid food? If so, be prepared to make a long-term commitment to learning to distinguish good from evil, truth from lies. You can be totally transformed as you choose to renew your mind.

Declaration

In Jesus' name we declare that God is sovereign in this place and over our lives and that we are here by legal right. And so we tell every enemy of the Lord Jesus Christ to be silent and leave this place immediately. You will not stop the will of God being done in this group.

Have you become aware during the course so far of any faulty beliefs or unhelpful patterns of behaviour you have had?

How optimistic are you that you can break free from these faulty beliefs and unhelpful patterns of behaviour and genuinely change? What do you think would need to happen for you to see real transformation in these areas?

Milk or meat?

Therefore, since we are surrounded by such a great cloud of witnesses, let us throw off everything that hinders and the sin that so easily entangles. And let us run with perseverance the race marked out for us, fixing our eyes on Jesus, the pioneer and perfecter of faith.

Hebrews 12:1-2

Therefore, I urge you, brothers and sisters, in view of God's mercy, to offer your bodies as a living sacrifice, holy and pleasing to God – this is your true and proper worship. Do not conform to the pattern of this world, but be transformed by the renewing of your mind. Then you will be able to test and approve what God's will is – his good, pleasing and perfect will.

Romans 12:1-2

Christians are meant to keep growing to maturity – and there's no reason why we can't – but it's not inevitable that we will.

We will be transformed as we renew our minds.

Uncovering lies and renewing our minds with truth needs to become a regular practice. "Stronghold-busting" (see pages 141–144 and the *disciple* app) is an effective way to do this.

Stronghold:

A deeply-rooted belief that is contrary to God's Word.

THE WEAPONS WE FIGHT WITH ARE
NOT THE WEAPONS OF THE WORLD.
ON THE CONTRARY, THEY HAVE DIVINE
POWER TO DEMOLISH STRONGHOLDS.
WE DEMOLISH ARGUMENTS AND
EVERY PRETENSION THAT SETS ITSELF
UP AGAINST THE KNOWLEDGE OF
GOD, AND WE TAKE CAPTIVE EVERY
THOUGHT TO MAKE IT OBEDIENT TO
CHRIST.

2 Corinthians 10:4-5

"Stronghold-Busting":
a practical way to renew your mind

1. Determine the lie you have been believing , that is to say any way you are thinking that is not in line with what God says about you in the Bible. In doing this, ignore what you feel but commit yourself wholeheartedly to God's truth.

2. Write down what effects believing the lie has had in your life. How different would your life be if you were to replace this lie with what is actually true?

3. Find as many Bible verses as you can that state the truth and write them down.

4. Write a prayer/declaration based on the formula:
    > I renounce the lie that...
    > I announce the truth that...

5. Finally, read the Bible verses and say the prayer/declaration out loud every day for forty days. You can set the *disciple* app to remind you each day.

Lasting change demands an intentional commitment to truth. Throughout much of this time, it will feel like you are wasting your time because the lie will *feel* true and the truth you are speaking from God's Word will *feel* unreal. However, if you persevere long enough (and it usually takes six weeks or so), your belief system *will* change and you will have been transformed through the renewing of your mind (Romans 12:2). Look at the examples on the following pages and then write your own stronghold-busters using the space on pages 146–151. Go for it!

Stronghold-Buster Example 1
Taking Comfort In Food Rather Than God

The lie: that overeating brings lasting comfort.

Effects in my life: harmful to health; becoming overweight; giving the enemy a foothold; stopping my growth to maturity

Proverbs 25:28: Like a city whose walls are broken down is a person who lacks self-control.

Galatians 5:16: So I say, walk by the Spirit, and you will not gratify the desires of the flesh.

Galatians 5:22–24: But the fruit of the Spirit is love, joy, peace, forbearance, kindness, goodness, faithfulness, gentleness and self-control. Against such things there is no law. Those who belong to Christ Jesus have crucified the flesh with its passions and desires.

2 Corinthians 1:3–4: Praise be to the God and Father of our Lord Jesus Christ, the Father of compassion and the God of all comfort, who comforts us in all our troubles, so that we can comfort those in any trouble with the comfort we ourselves receive from God.

Psalm 63:4–5: I will praise you as long as I live, and in your name I will lift up my hands. I will be fully satisfied as with the richest of foods; with singing lips my mouth will praise you.

Psalm 119:76: May your unfailing love be my comfort.

God, I renounce the lie that overeating brings lasting comfort. I announce the truth that you are the God of all comfort and that your unfailing love is my only legitimate and real comfort. I affirm that I now live by the Spirit and do not have to gratify the desires of the flesh. Whenever I feel in need of comfort, instead of turning to foods I choose to praise you and be satisfied as with the richest of foods. Fill me afresh with your Holy Spirit and live through me as I grow in self-control. Amen.

Mark off the days:

1	2	3	4	5	6	7	8	9
10	11	12	13	14	15	16	17	18
19	20	21	22	23	24	25	26	27
28	29	30	31	32	33	34	35	36
37	38	39	40					

Stronghold-Buster Example 2
Always Feeling Alone

The lie: that I am abandoned and forgotten.

Effects in my life: withdrawing from others; thinking people don't like me; seeming aloof; frightened

Deuteronomy 31:6: Be strong and courageous. Do not be afraid or terrified because of them, for the LORD your God goes with you; he will never leave you nor forsake you.

Isaiah 46:4: Even to your old age and grey hairs I am he, I am he who will sustain you. I have made you and I will carry you; I will sustain you and I will rescue you.

Jeremiah 29:11: "For I know the plans I have for you," declares the LORD, "plans to prosper you and not to harm you, plans to give you hope and a future."

Romans 8:37–38: For I am convinced that neither death nor life, neither angels nor demons, neither the present nor the future, nor any powers, neither height nor depth, nor anything else in all creation, will be able to separate us from the love of God that is in Christ Jesus our Lord.

Dear Heavenly Father

I renounce the lie that I am abandoned and forgotten and will be left on my own.

I announce the truth that you love me, that you have plans to give me a hope and a future and that absolutely nothing can separate me from your love.

In Jesus' name. Amen.

Mark off the days:

1	2	3	4	5	6	7	8	9
10	11	12	13	14	15	16	17	18
19	20	21	22	23	24	25	26	27
28	29	30	31	32	33	34	35	36
37	38	39	40					

Stronghold-Buster Example 3
Feeling Irresistibly Drawn To Internet Porn

The lie: that I cannot resist the temptation to look at internet porn.

Effects in my life: deep sense of shame; warped sexual feelings; unable to relate to other people as God intended; harmful to my marriage

Romans 6:11–14: In the same way, count yourselves dead to sin but alive to God in Christ Jesus. Therefore do not let sin reign in your mortal body so that you obey its evil desires. Do not offer the parts of your body to sin, as instruments of wickedness, but rather offer yourselves to God, as those who have been brought from death to life; and offer every part of yourself to him as an instrument of righteousness. For sin shall not be your master, because you are not under the law, but under grace.

1 Corinthians 6:19: Do you not know that your bodies are temples of the Holy Spirit?

1 Corinthians 10:13: No temptation has overtaken you except what is common to mankind. And God is faithful; he will not let you be tempted beyond what you can bear. But when you are tempted, he will also provide a way out so that you can endure it.

Galatians 5:16: So I say, live by the Spirit, and you will not gratify the desires of the flesh.

Galatians 5:22–23: But the fruit of the Spirit is love, joy, peace, forbearance, kindness, goodness, faithfulness, gentleness and self-control.

I renounce the lie that I cannot resist the temptation to look at internet porn. I declare the truth that God will always provide a way out when I am tempted and I will choose to take it. I announce the truth that if I live by the Spirit – and I choose to do that – I will not gratify the desires of the flesh and the fruit of the Spirit, including self-control, will grow in me. I count myself dead to sin and refuse to let sin reign in my body or be my master. Today and every day I give my body to God as a temple of the Holy Spirit to be used only for what honours Him. I declare that the power of sin is broken in me. I choose to submit completely to God and resist the devil who must flee from me now.

Mark off the days:

1	2	3	4	5	6	7	8	9
10	11	12	13	14	15	16	17	18
19	20	21	22	23	24	25	26	27
28	29	30	31	32	33	34	35	36
37	38	39	40					

Chat

Take the biggest lie you realize you have fallen for (look at the list you have made on pages 190–191) and construct a stronghold-buster that you can use to tear it down over the next forty days or so. There is space on pages 146–147 for you to do this (and further space on the following four pages for you to put together other stronghold-busters in the future). You could also construct it in the app.

If you are struggling to think of a lie to tackle, you could pick one from this list of typical lies that Christians have come to believe:

- I am unloved
- I am a failure
- Life is hopeless
- I can never change
- God will not provide for my needs
- This will work for others but my case is special.

If you need some help to find the truth from God's Word, the "Truth Encounter" lists from Sessions 2, 3, and 8 are likely to be a good source of inspiration. If you don't have time to complete it, finish it at home.

Remember to check out the Stronghold-Buster section of the *disciple* app where you can record your stronghold-buster and set up daily reminders.

Is there someone you could encourage every day to go through their stronghold-buster?

1. What lie do you want to tackle?

2. What effect does this faulty belief have on your life? How different would your life be if you replaced it with what is actually true?

3. List below as many Bible verses as you can that state what God says is actually true:

4. Write a prayer/declaration:

I RENOUNCE the lie that

I ANNOUNCE the tRUth that

5. Read the Bible verses and say the prayer/declaration out loud every day for forty days. You can set the *disciple* app to remind you each day. Mark off the days below:

1	2	3	4	5	6	7	8	9
10	11	12	13	14	15	16	17	18
19	20	21	22	23	24	25	26	27
28	29	30	31	32	33	34	35	36
37	38	39	40					

1. What lie do you want to tackle?

2. What effect does this faulty belief have on your life? How different would your life be if you replaced it with what is actually true?

3. List below as many Bible verses as you can that state what God says is actually true:

4. **Write a prayer/declaration:**

I Renounce the lie that

I announce the truth that

5. **Read the Bible verses and say the prayer/declaration out loud every day for forty days. You can set the *disciple* app to remind you each day. Mark off the days below:**

1	2	3	4	5	6	7	8	9
10	11	12	13	14	15	16	17	18
19	20	21	22	23	24	25	26	27
28	29	30	31	32	33	34	35	36
37	38	39	40					

My Stronghold-Buster 3

1. What lie do you want to tackle?

2. What effect does this faulty belief have on your life? How different would your life be if you replaced it with what is actually true?

3. List below as many Bible verses as you can that state what God says is actually true:

4. Write a prayer/declaration:

I renounce the lie that

I announce the truth that

5. Read the Bible verses and say the prayer/declaration out loud every
   day for forty days. You can set the *disciple* app to remind you each day.
   Mark off the days below:

1	2	3	4	5	6	7	8	9
10	11	12	13	14	15	16	17	18
19	20	21	22	23	24	25	26	27
28	29	30	31	32	33	34	35	36
37	38	39	40					

The goal

> Praise be to the God and Father of our Lord Jesus Christ, who has blessed us in the heavenly realms with every spiritual blessing in Christ.
>
> **Ephesians 1:3**

The goals we have developed for life may be good but if they can be blocked by others they set us up for problems;

- anxiety shows an uncertain goal
- anger shows a blocked goal
- depression can show a failed or unreachable goal

If God has a goal for your life, by definition it must be achievable. God would not ask you to do something that you couldn't do.

We can conclude that God's goal for our lives is that we become more and more like Jesus in character. He is primarily concerned with what we are *like* rather than what we *do*.

Bringing our goals into line with this will prevent a lot of anxiety, anger, and depression (but see the note on depression on page 109).

HIS DIVINE POWER HAS GIVEN US EVERYTHING
WE NEED FOR A GODLY LIFE THROUGH OUR
KNOWLEDGE OF HIM WHO CALLED US BY
HIS OWN GLORY AND GOODNESS. THROUGH
THESE HE HAS GIVEN US HIS VERY GREAT AND
PRECIOUS PROMISES, SO THAT THROUGH
THEM YOU MAY PARTICIPATE IN THE DIVINE
NATURE, HAVING ESCAPED THE CORRUPTION
IN THE WORLD CAUSED BY EVIL DESIRES.

FOR THIS VERY REASON, MAKE EVERY
EFFORT TO ADD TO YOUR FAITH GOODNESS;
AND TO GOODNESS, KNOWLEDGE; AND
TO KNOWLEDGE, SELF-CONTROL; AND TO
SELF-CONTROL, PERSEVERANCE; AND
TO PERSEVERANCE, GODLINESS; AND TO
GODLINESS, MUTUAL AFFECTION; AND
TO MUTUAL AFFECTION, LOVE. FOR IF YOU
POSSESS THESE QUALITIES IN INCREASING
MEASURE, THEY WILL KEEP YOU FROM BEING
INEFFECTIVE AND UNPRODUCTIVE IN YOUR
KNOWLEDGE OF OUR LORD JESUS CHRIST.

2 Peter 1:3-8 (ESV)

153

Goals – follow the logic...

A "goal" (in the way we are using the term in this session) is something that is so important to you, that you feel your very sense of success or failure as a person depends on achieving it.

If your goal feels:

uncertain	it leads to	**anxiety;**
blocked	it leads to	**anger;**
unachievable	it leads to	**depression.**

But God would not ask you to do something you cannot do. So by definition **no God-given goal can be uncertain, blocked, or unachievable.**

Therefore, any goal that can be blocked by people or circumstances beyond your control is not a goal God wants you to have.

It may still be a good thing in itself so you don't have to abandon it. Just downgrade it from a <u>goal</u> to a <u>desire</u>. In other words don't let it determine your sense of who you are. If it doesn't happen, yes, it's a disappointment. But it's not a disaster.

Rather, adopt God's goal for your life: **to become more and more like Jesus in character.** Nothing and no one can block that goal – except you!

If you're honest, do you feel you're lacking something you need to become a fruitful disciple? If so, what?

Are you able to pinpoint goals that you unconsciously developed for your life, goals that you thought would make you happy or fulfilled? What were they? Why are goals that depend on the cooperation of other people or favourable circumstances unhealthy?

"God is primarily concerned with what you are like rather than what you do." What practical difference might it make in your life to realize that God's goal for you is to grow in character rather than to accomplish something specific?

Relationship not religion

> And let us consider how we may spur one another on toward love and good deeds, not giving up meeting together, as some are in the habit of doing, but encouraging one another – and all the more as you see the Day approaching.
>
> **Hebrews 10:24-25**

Although God is primarily concerned with what you are *like*, He also cares hugely about what you *do*. The big idea is that He knows that what you do will come from who you are. "The root bears the fruit" – the more like Jesus you are, the more your actions will reflect Him.

Walking with God means inviting him into our entire life.

"I alone cannot change the world but I can cast a stone that makes many ripples" – Mother Teresa

We can all leave a mark on the earth and build that treasure in heaven.

We need to be part of the body of Christ.

Reflect

Does it shock you to think that God hates religion? Ask Him to show you if any of things you do as a Christian come from a sense of religion rather than relationship.

Being a disciple is about having a real relationship with God Himself, the Creator of everything. What words would you use to describe your relationship with God right now? Tell Him your hopes and dreams for your future relationship with Him.

Are you a committed member of the Christian community? If not, ask someone to pray with you before you leave that God will show you exactly the place for you to serve and flourish.

God may still be using *disciple* to help you see areas in your belief system that are not in line with what He says is true. Continue to write them down on pages 190–191 together with the corresponding truth.

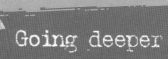

Going deeper

Take some quiet time with God on your own where you have no agenda other than seeking Him and being with Him. It might help to have some worship music and your Bible. Remember to switch off your phone and be ready to make notes of anything He may show you.

Start doing your first stronghold-buster this week and bear in mind that, in order to get to the end and see transformation in your life, it will take perseverance and effort. It will, however, be well worth it!

NEXT TIME

In our final session we will look at what God is inviting you to do with the rest of your story – prepare to be surprised!

- Being Jesus' ambassador
- Our amazing mandate to bring transformation
- What lasts for ever.

disciple: the journey continues...

10

Action story

WHY?

"For I know the plans I have for you," declares the Lord, "plans to prosper you and not to harm you, plans to give you hope and a future."

Jeremiah 29:11

God is God. He doesn't need us to work with Him to fulfil His incredible plan for the world. Yet He chooses to partner with us and entrust us with a staggering mandate: to bring transformation to the world around us. We are ambassadors for Christ and can choose to offer our lives to God so that we make an eternal difference.

Declaration

We declare that Jesus Christ came to destroy all of the works of the devil. The One who is in us is greater than the one who is in the world. As children of God, we declare that the devil cannot steal, kill, or destroy what God has planned to do among us today. Neither can he stop God's plans for the rest of our lives.

STARTER
FILM

What is the best invitation you have ever received?

How does it make you feel to know that God invites you to join in with His work but puts you under no pressure whatsoever to do so?

God chose you and you are free to choose

"You did not choose me, but I chose you and appointed you so that you might go and bear fruit – fruit that will last."

John 15:16

God has chosen to make known among the Gentiles the glorious riches of this mystery, which is Christ in you, the hope of glory.

Colossians 1:27

For we are God's handiwork, created in Christ Jesus to do good works, which God prepared in advance for us to do.

Ephesians 2:10

God really did choose <u>you</u>! Whether you know it or not, your potential is enormous.

What you do comes from who you are.

You are in Christ:
- You are a new creation
- You are a minister of reconciliation
- You are Jesus' ambassador.

Christ is in you:
- He literally lives in you through His Spirit
- You already have everything you need to be a fruitful disciple.

THEREFORE, IF ANYONE IS IN CHRIST, THE NEW CREATION HAS COME: THE OLD HAS GONE, THE NEW IS HERE! ALL THIS IS FROM GOD, WHO RECONCILED US TO HIMSELF THROUGH CHRIST AND GAVE US THE MINISTRY OF RECONCILIATION: THAT GOD WAS RECONCILING THE WORLD TO HIMSELF IN CHRIST, NOT COUNTING PEOPLE'S SINS AGAINST THEM.

AND HE HAS COMMITTED TO US THE MESSAGE OF RECONCILIATION. WE ARE THEREFORE CHRIST'S AMBASSADORS, AS THOUGH GOD WERE MAKING HIS APPEAL THROUGH US. WE IMPLORE YOU ON CHRIST'S BEHALF: BE RECONCILED TO GOD.

GOD MADE HIM WHO HAD NO SIN TO **BE** SIN FOR US, SO THAT IN HIM WE MIGHT **BECOME** THE RIGHTEOUSNESS OF GOD.

2 Corinthians 5:17-21

If anyone builds on this foundation using gold, silver, costly stones, wood, hay or straw, his work will be shown for what it is, because the Day will bring it to light. It will be revealed with fire, and the fire will test the quality of each person's work. If what has been built survives, the builder will receive his reward. If it is burned up, the builder will suffer loss; but yet will be saved – even though only as one escaping through the flames.

1 Corinthians 3:12–15

What you do will be tested in the end – But God loves you whether you use your life to make an eternal difference or not.

There is no pressure. You have complete freedom to choose how your story goes on from here – do you want to build treasure in heaven that will last for ever or are you content with treasure on earth that is here today but will be gone tomorrow?

Chat

disciple

Think back to what you said you wanted from the rest of your life when you started *disciple* (look back at what you wrote on page 16). Has it changed at all? If so, how and why?

What difference does knowing that you are Christ's ambassador make to you?

How does the fact that Christ is <u>in</u> you change the way you feel about following your calling and your expectations of what might happen in your life from this point on?

Always be prepared to give an answer to everyone who asks you to give the reason for the hope that you have. But do this with gentleness and respect.

1 Peter 3:15

After they prayed, the place where they were meeting was shaken. And they were all filled with the Holy Spirit and spoke the word of God boldly.

Acts 4:31

Jesus read the passage on the opposite page (see Luke 4:16–20) and finished by saying: "Today this scripture is fulfilled in your hearing." This was His mandate.

We are the Body of Christ – the actual flesh and blood through whom He works in the world. Therefore, we share Jesus' mandate to:

- proclaim the good news
- bring justice, righteousness, freedom, and transformation to our world.

Disciples of Jesus:

- Just need to be themselves
- Are prepared to give an answer
- Pray for boldness
- Live a counter-cultural existence
- Help others find true freedom.

THE SPIRIT OF THE SOVEREIGN LORD
IS ON ME, BECAUSE THE LORD HAS
ANOINTED ME TO PROCLAIM GOOD
NEWS TO THE POOR. HE HAS SENT ME
TO BIND UP THE BROKEN HEARTED, TO
PROCLAIM FREEDOM FOR THE CAPTIVES
AND RELEASE FROM DARKNESS FOR THE
PRISONERS, TO PROCLAIM THE YEAR OF
THE LORD'S FAVOUR AND THE DAY OF
VENGEANCE OF OUR GOD, TO COMFORT
ALL WHO MOURN, AND PROVIDE FOR
THOSE WHO GRIEVE IN ZION – TO BESTOW
ON THEM A CROWN OF BEAUTY INSTEAD
OF ASHES, THE OIL OF JOY INSTEAD
OF MOURNING, AND A GARMENT
OF PRAISE INSTEAD OF A SPIRIT OF
DESPAIR. THEY WILL BE CALLED OAKS
OF RIGHTEOUSNESS, A PLANTING OF
THE LORD FOR THE DISPLAY OF HIS
SPLENDOUR.

Isaiah 61:1-3

Chat

disciple

What are some of the reasons that it can seem so hard to share about Jesus with our not-yet-Christian friends? How can we overcome our fear?

How do you feel about the truth that you are literally the flesh and blood that Jesus chooses to work through in the world? What alternative plans might God have to get His work done if we choose not to play our part (see Esther 4:14)?

Read Isaiah 61:1–3 (see previous page). If this is our mandate, what would you say are God's priorities for His people?

So, what will you choose?

Because of the crowd he told his disciples to have a small boat ready for him, to keep the people from crowding him. For he had healed many, so that those with diseases were pushing forward to touch him.

Jesus went up on a mountainside and called to him those he wanted, and they came to him. He appointed twelve that they might be with him and that he might send them out to preach and to have authority to drive out demons.

Mark 3:9–10, 13–15

Realizing who we now are changes everything!

God is inviting us to join in with His story.

We don't have to respond to His invitation. He will love us whatever we choose. It all comes down to whether we want our lives to count for eternity, whether we want to make a real difference or not.

Will we settle for being just part of the crowd coming to Jesus for what we can get? Or, will we choose to be radical disciples, committed to fulfilling our mandate in the power of the Holy Spirit?

Reflect

What is the main thing you will take away from *disciple*?

How confident do you feel that God can use you to advance His purpose and to make a real difference that will have an eternal impact?

Pair up and pray for each other's onward journey in life as fruitful disciples who are making a difference.

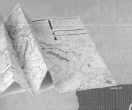

Going deeper

- Ask God to show you what it means to be an ambassador for Him where He has placed you.
- Ask God to show you where there are injustices in the place He has put you and what you can do about them.

Don't forget to keep going with that stronghold-buster!

Oh... you didn't start it? No problem! Just start today. You missed a day? Don't worry – God is not cross with you! This is not some religious duty, it's a life-transforming process. Do it because you want to be different and make a difference. Just pick up where you left off and keep going until you know that you believe the truth.

EXTRA FILM

ON THE APP

OVERCOMING FEAR AND TAKING A RISK FOR JESUS

A whole new beginning

So you have come to the end of *disciple*! But this is not the end of your story. In fact it's a whole new beginning, and for that reason we have given you extra pages to journal your ongoing journey from here. Do stay in touch with us through our Facebook group. We would love to see how your story is unfolding.

We hope that you have enjoyed travelling through *disciple* and that it has given you not just the inspiration and freedom to make your life count for eternity but a practical tool kit to make it happen.

We recommend that you go through *The Steps To Freedom In Christ* once a year as a kind of spiritual health check. You don't necessarily need an organized Steps day or Steps appointment. You can take each other through or even take yourself through now that the big clean-up is done!

We want to remind you that transformation does not come through trying harder or even through getting people to pray for you. It comes through renewing your mind and no one else can do that for you. It's essential that you take responsibility to continue to deal with faulty beliefs that God shows you. Keep going with those stronghold-busters even though they 'feel' pointless!

Your ongoing daily relationship with God is key. Keep talking to Him and simply enjoy being with Him with no pressure to "perform" or do anything! There is no set way to pray but we thought we would share some useful prayers (on the following pages) to start you off. Do make them your own and pray them from your heart. Remember they are not magic mantras – it's about growing in your relationship with God, not how "good" your prayers are.

Prepare to be amazed as your Heavenly Father who loves you so much unfolds more and more of His purposes for your life. What an exciting read it's going to be!

Daily prayer and declaration

Dear Heavenly Father,

Thank You that You are my Lord and Saviour and that You are in control of everything. Thank You that You're always with me and never leave me or let me go. You are the only all-powerful and wise God. You are kind and loving in every way. I love You and thank You that I am in Jesus and spiritually alive in Him. I choose today not to love the world or the world's things, and I crucify the flesh and its passions.

Thank You for the life I have in Jesus. Please fill me with the Holy Spirit so I can say no to sin and yes to You. I know that I am totally dependent on You and I take my stand against Satan and all his lies.

I choose to believe the truth of your Word not my feelings. I refuse to be discouraged; You are the God of all hope. Nothing is too difficult for You. You will meet all my needs as I choose to live by the truth of Your Word. Thank You that I can be content and live responsibly through Jesus who gives me strength.

I submit to God and take my stand against Satan and command him and all his evil spirits to leave me. I put on the whole armour of God and choose to stand firm against all the devil's schemes.

I surrender my body to You, Lord God, as a living and holy sacrifice and I choose to renew my mind by Your Word,.

I declare that I am a new creation, a holy one, a disciple of Jesus, an ambassador of Christ, and one through whom God Himself will bring righteousness, truth, and justice.

Thank You that Your plans are good, pleasing, and perfect for me.

I pray confidently as a child of God in the name of Jesus.

Amen.

Bedtime prayer

Thank You, Father God, that I am part of Your family and that You have blessed me with every spiritual blessing in Jesus.

Thank You for this time of sleep to be renewed and refreshed. I thank you for sleep as one of Your blessings for Your children and I trust You to guard my mind and my body while I am sleeping.

As I have thought about You and Your truth today, I choose to let those good thoughts stay with me while I am asleep. I trust You to protect me against every attempt of Satan and his demons to attack me while I sleep. I submit to God and command every enemy of the Lord Jesus Christ to leave my presence.

Please guard me from nightmares. I renounce all fear and cast every anxiety upon You. I specifically give you my anxieties about _____ (list them), Father. I commit myself wholeheartedly and unreservedly to You as my rock and my fortress. Please bless this place of rest with your peace now.

I pray in the name of Jesus with confidence that You love me and have heard me. Thank you!

Amen.

Extra films

Why believe the Bible?

There are six extra films to help you look at various aspects of the course in a little more detail. Access them from the *disciple* app (see page 7).

> All Scripture is God-breathed and is useful for teaching, rebuking, correcting and training in righteousness, so that the servant of God may be thoroughly equipped for every good work.
>
> **2 Timothy 3:16–17**

Archaeology consistently backs up the Bible's accounts.

The Bible also proves its own contents. There are over 300 prophecies that came true about the life of Jesus alone.

Changed lives point to the truth of the Bible.

The Church keeps growing. Jesus said, "I will build my church" (Matthew 16:18) and He's been doing that ever since. There are almost certainly more Christians alive right now than have ever lived and died throughout the whole of history!

The gift of sex

That is why a man leaves his father and mother and is united to his wife, and they become one flesh. Adam and his wife were both naked, and they felt no shame.

Genesis 2:24-25

Do you not know that your bodies are members of Christ himself? Shall I then take the members of Christ and unite them with a prostitute? Never! Do you not know that he who unites himself with a prostitute is one with her in body? For it is said, "The two will become one flesh." But whoever is united with the Lord is one with him in spirit.

1 Corinthians 6:15-17

Part 1: As God intended

Sex is good! It was there in the Garden of Eden before sin entered the world.

The context God has created for sex is a committed relationship between a man and a woman, and specifically a marriage relationship where the commitment is affirmed before God and before other people.

Sex is not just a physical act but a spiritual act designed to bond a man and wife together. Sex outside marriage has the consequence of forming an unhelpful spiritual bond.

Being single is just as significant as being married.

No matter what your sexual history, God offers you total cleansing, forgiveness, and a brand new start.

Part 2: Pornography and masturbation
Porn and masturbation may feel like harmless fun but they can become snares that are hard to break free from. They are by nature addictive.

Porn exploits people and is essentially selfish in its expression.

Masturbation is all about self-gratification rather than an intimate union which takes account of both parties' need for intimacy. It can be hard to move from "my" needs and desires to "your" and "our" needs and desires.

Porn and masturbation can leave you open to spiritual attack and feeling ashamed and powerless.

God can set you free from any sexual bondage as you submit to Him, resist the devil, and commit to renew your mind.

The truth behind the occult

When you enter the land the Lord your God is giving you, do not learn to imitate the detestable ways of the nations there. Let no one be found among you who sacrifices their son or daughter in the fire, who practises divination or sorcery, interprets omens, engages in witchcraft, or casts spells, or who is a medium or spiritist or who consults the dead. Anyone who does these things is detestable to the Lord; because of these same detestable practices the Lord your God will drive out those nations before you.

Deuteronomy 18:9–12

Every spirit that acknowledges that Jesus Christ has come in the flesh is from God, but every spirit that does not acknowledge Jesus is not from God. This is the spirit of the antichrist.

1 John 4:2–3

The lure of the occult is to do with getting knowledge, power, healing, or peace. Of course all that can be found in God and what Satan offers are counterfeits. Nothing gives him more of a claim on you than if you dabble in the occult.

Satan cannot read your mind and does not know the future (other than what God has revealed).

The New Age movement takes spiritual practices from other religions and is at the foundation of widely accepted self-help courses, business training, and even some types of medicine. Things like guided imagery and meditation are widely accepted in workplaces, schools, and even churches. They may seem harmless but they aren't.

It is straightforward to resolve past dabbling in the occult using *The Steps To Freedom In Christ*. You submit to God by admitting that you have done it and agreeing never to do it again and then you resist the devil by claiming back the ground you gave him in your life – and he will flee, very undramatically and quietly (see James 4:7).

God, my Father

> But when the set time had fully come, God sent his Son, born of a woman, born under the law, to redeem those under the law, that we might receive adoption to sonship. Because you are his sons, God sent the Spirit of his Son into our hearts, the Spirit who calls out, "Abba, Father."
>
> **Galatians 4:4–7**

God is the source and the originator of your life. He really is your father and absolutely nothing can change that.

God loves you because He <u>is</u> love. (1 John 4:8).

Through your faith in Jesus Christ, you have been adopted by God. In Roman law adoption to SONSHIP meant:

- You have the right to the name and the citizenship of the person who adopted you
- You have the right to inherit their property
- You have the same rights and privileges as if you were a naturally born son.

God is interested in every aspect of your life and development (see Jeremiah 29:11). He wants you to be all that you can be and He has given you everything you need to become a growing disciple whose life will count for eternity.

As you choose to trust Him with every aspect of your life, He will guide you. Sometimes He will discipline you out of love (see Hebrews 12:6) to help you learn not to make the same mistake again.

God will never leave you or let you down (see Hebrews 13:5).

To get these truths from head to heart:
1. Make a choice not to let your past experiences define you.
2. Forgive and keep forgiving.
3. Be transformed through the renewal of your mind.

Overcoming fear and taking a risk for Jesus

God gave us a spirit not of fear but of power, love and self-control.

2 Timothy 1:7 (ESV)

There is no fear in love, but perfect love casts out fear. For fear has to do with punishment, and whoever fears has not been perfected in love.

1 John 4:18 (ESV)

The risk of not taking a risk – forty years in the wilderness for the Israelites. Joshua and Caleb were willing to risk everything because they "wholly followed the Lord." They understood their identity and by faith were willing to claim what was promised.

Fear is a gift from God designed to keep us safe. For a fear to be healthy the thing you fear needs to be present (near you) and powerful (able to do you harm). If the thing you are fearing is not near you or not able to do you harm it's an unhealthy fear.

Overcoming unhealthy fear in our lives:

1. Identify sin areas in our lives where we are choosing to yield to FEAR rather than trust and love. *The Steps To Freedom In Christ* will help you do that.
2. Acknowledge that God is always with you and that He has all power and authority.
3. Work out the lie behind the fear.
4. Counter that fear as you trust in God and choose to believe the truth. A stronghold-buster will help you replace the lie with truth.

Submit yourselves, then, to God. Resist the devil, and he will flee from you.

James 4:7

In *disciple* we teach a way of life that, if you follow it, will lead to you making a huge impact for God. There are three elements to this way of life:

1. Understand who you really are in Christ, that you are a holy one, that God delights in you.
2. Use the power and authority you have as a child of God to take back any ground you've given to the enemy through any past mistakes.
3. Keep being transformed by the renewing of your mind as you throw out lies and choose to believe the truth.

The Steps To Freedom In Christ is a small book written by Neil Anderson that helps you put into practice the second element. It leads you through prayers concerning seven areas of your life. It is simply a tool to help you come before Jesus and ask Him to show you any issues that are holding you back and deal with them.

You are completely in control. You choose which prayers you need to pray. It's all just between you and God. If you deal with everything He shows you, you will be free. But it's not the Steps that sets you free. It's Jesus!

This is not a one-off process but a tool that you can pull out again and again whenever you need it. We recommend going through the Steps at least once a year.

Faulty Thinking (Lies)	What God Says (Truth)

Faulty Thinking (Lies)	What God Says (Truth)

Join us and equip more churches to make fruitful disciples!

"Can you think of anything more worthwhile than helping every Christian become a fruitful disciple? At Freedom In Christ that's our passion! The impact we're seeing is breathtaking, and it's an incredibly exciting story to be part of.

"Now that you have finished *disciple*, what's next? What's your God-given mandate? There's a wealth of exciting opportunities out there to get stuck into in God's Kingdom.

"But if you're as excited as I am about the global impact of a Church truly free and fruitful, I'd love you to consider partnering with us at Freedom In Christ Ministries.

"With your regular support, we can continue to develop resources that make fruitful disciples – resources for children, youth, parents, marriages, those who are badly hurting, and those who desperately need to know who they are in Christ.

"You can help us get those resources into more churches, more communities, and more families. We can see more Christians, families, and churches all around the world firmly established in the freedom that Jesus has won for them, becoming fruitful and transforming the lives of those around them. Your regular gift can make a massive difference."

To partner with us in your country, head to:
FICMinternational.org/partner and join us in the *disciple* story.